RELIGIOUS CONFLICT IN AMERICA

GARLAND REFERENCE LIBRARY
OF SOCIAL SCIENCE
(VOL. 262)

RELIGIOUS CONFLICT IN AMERICA
A Bibliography

Albert J. Menendez

GARLAND PUBLISHING, INC. • NEW YORK & LONDON
1985

Library of Congress Cataloging in Publication Data

Menendez, Albert J.
Religious conflict in America.

(Garland reference library of social science ; v. 262)
Includes index.
1. United States—Religion—Bibliography.   2. Church
and state—United States—Bibliography.   I. Title.
II. Series.
Z7757.U5M46   1985   [BR515]   016.2911′72′0973   84-13779
ISBN 0-8240-8904-9 (alk. paper)

Cover design by Laurence Walczak

Printed on acid-free, 250-year-life paper
Manufactured in the United States of America

For Shirley

CONTENTS

INTRODUCTION

Religious conflict is as American as apple pie. No one likes to admit it today but it is a burdensome truth. Conflicts among religious groups or between religious groups and the government have been a persistent problem throughout U.S. history.

Since profound ignorance of this subject seems endemic in America today, I have prepared this bibliographic guide to the literature. Though selective, it incorporates the major writings which deal with religious conflict and hostility throughout three centuries. Both secondary and primary source materials are included. Books, periodical articles, law review treatises, doctoral dissertations, masters' theses, and a few newspaper articles have been included. The focus is primarily historical, though sociological interpretations have also been cited. Purely theological articles have generally been omitted, except where they clearly impinge on the political or cultural setting.

My approach has generally been chronological, beginning with the various forms of religious repression which existed in colonial America and ending with calendar year 1983. This enables the student of this subject to perceive the ebbs and flows of interfaith conflict.

Political conflict along religious lines has been a principal, if not primary, arena of controversy between religious bodies. Therefore, my next sections (H through K) focus on the campaigns for the Presidency and the religious issues which accompanied them.

Next, I move to several areas where conflict has always been intense: organized movements to convert those of a rival faith, the clash over public aid to church-related schools, and the role of religion in the public schools.

To make this study as up-to-date as possible, I have also included a small section on that amorphous entity known as "civil religion" and on the relatively new phenomenon of cults and religious deprogramming. This bibliography concludes with 101 items on the Reagan Presidency and its involvement with right-wing religious forces—an ominous development which bodes ill for the preservation of religious liberty in America.

Religious Conflict in America

SECTION A
GENERAL STUDIES OF RELIGIOUS CONFLICT IN AMERICA,
INCLUDING SOME GENERAL BIBLIOGRAPHIES OF U.S. RELIGIOUS HISTORY

Religious conflict in United States history is shrouded in secrecy. It is almost nonexistent in elementary and secondary school textbooks, and rarely noted in college-level ones. Even knowledgeable and otherwise well-informed Americans know little of the struggle for religious liberty and freedom of conscience on our soil during the past four centuries.

A good place to sample the flavor of the subject is A7, which is angry and flamboyant in tone. A6 and A3 should be read next. The essays in A9 are especially useful for the political context. Perhaps the pre-eminent volume is A8. A good, brief overview can be found in A4.

A1 Burr, Nelson R. A Critical Bibliography of Religion in America. Princeton: Princeton University Press, 1961.

A2 Burr, Nelson R. Religion in American Life. New York: Appleton-Century-Crofts, 1971.

A3 Clinchy, Everett Ross. All in the Name of God. New York: The John Day Company, 1934.

A4 Hager, D. J. "Religious Conflict in the United States." Journal of Social Issues 12 (1956): 1-66.

A5 Kane, John J. Catholic-Protestant Conflicts in America. Chicago: Henry Regnery, 1955.

A6 Maury, Reuben. The Wars of the Godly: The Story of Religious Conflict in America. New York: McBride, 1928.

A7 Menendez, Albert J. "Who Said It Can't Happen Here?" Liberty 73 (March-April 1978): 4-8.

A8 Meyers, Gustavus. History of Bigotry in the United States. New York: Capricorn, 1943.

A9 Raab, Earl, ed. Religious Conflict in America. New York: Doubleday, 1964.

A10 Vollmar, Edward R. The Catholic Church in America, A Descriptive Bibliography. New York: Scarecrow Press, 1963

SECTION B
RELIGIOUS CONFLICT IN COLONIAL AMERICA AND IN
THE EARLY NATIONAL PERIOD 1565-1830

Colonial America, being an extension of European church-states, was hardly enlightened in religious matters. Only two of the thirteen original colonies, Rhode Island and Pennsylvania, had any semblance of religious freedom, thanks in large measure to their Baptist and Quaker founders. Early Catholic Maryland had a brief experience in toleration. But all of the colonies experienced intolerance, religions established by law, and frequent discrimination against religious minorities. Quakers were hanged in Massachusetts and Catholics were executed in New York. Both groups were persecuted almost everywhere, as were Baptists.

The first religious martyrdom in America, that of the Spanish in Florida, is described in B44.

For an understanding of the context of anti-Catholicism, see B34, the best overall introduction available. B7 gives a frightening factual portrait of religious discrimination in colonial legislative and judicial acts. Even relatively tolerant Pennsylvania limited public office to Protestants, says B39. (See also B3-B5, B9, B10, B35 and B43.)

A good introduction to the development of religious freedom and the rights of conscience in the colonies can be found in B40 and B41. Sweet is often called the "dean of American church history."

Virginia was an important battleground in the travail of human rights. B27 is a superb collection of primary source documents, including previously unpublished manuscripts and letters, mostly from Baptist sources. For a more popular treatment of the same period, see B8, written by a Virginia historian and biographer of Jefferson Davis and several Confederate generals.

The battle to disestablish the churches in New England is recorded superbly in B11, B24, B26, B31, B36, and B43.

An attempt to whitewash and downplay religious intolerance can be found in B29.

Historians can be grateful to Johns Hopkins Press, which in the 1890s published a series of "studies in historical and political science." Many of these volumes were devoted to church-state relations. (See B26, B33, B42, and B45.)

Political anti-Catholicism is the primary issue addressed in B2, B3, B4, B5, B10, B12, B17, B22, B30, B32, B35, and B46. Political anti-Semitism is the focus for B1.

B1   Altfeld, E. Milton. The Jews' Struggle for Religious and
     Civil Liberty in Maryland. Baltimore: M. Curlander, 1924.

B2   "Anti-Catholic Movements in the United States." Catholic
     World 22 (1875): 810-822.

B3   Bosworth, Timothy W. "Anti-Catholicism as a Political Tool
     in Mid-Eighteenth Century Maryland." Catholic Historical
     Review 61 (1975): 535-563.

B4   Brady, Sister Eleanor Marie. "Anti-Catholic Legislation in
     Massachusetts Bay Colony." M.A. thesis. Villanova
     University, 1939.

B5   Casino, Joseph J. "Anti-Popery in Colonial Pennsylvania."
     Pennsylvania History 48 (1981): 51-61.

B6   Cudahy, Sister Eutropia. "Religious Liberty in Maryland Prior
     to the Act 1649." M.A. thesis. Marquette University, 1948.

B7   Curran, Charles. Catholics in Colonial Law. Chicago:
     Loyola University, 1963.

B8   Eckenrode, H. J. Separation of Church and State in Virginia.
     Richmond: Virginia State Library, 1910. (Reprint by
     Da Capo Press, 1971).

B9   Fitzgerald, Bernard M. "History of Religious Disqualifications
     for Office in Hew Hampshire." M.A. thesis. Catholic
     University, 1923.

B10 Fitzgerald, Frederick E. "Politico-Religious Discrimination
     Against Catholics in the Early Constitutions of the
     Southland, 1776-1835." M.A. thesis. Catholic University,
     1928.

B11 Ford, David B. New England's Struggle for Religious Liberty.
     Philadelphia: American Baptist Publication Society, 1896.

B12 Griffin, Martin I. J. "The Anti-Catholic Spirit of the
     Revolution." American Catholic Historical Researches
     6 (1889): 140-178.

B13 Griffin, Martin I. J. "William Penn, the Friend of Catholics."
     American Catholic Historical Society of Philadelphia Records
     1 (1884): 71-85.

B14 Hanley, Thomas O'Brien. "Church and State in the Maryland
     Ordinance of 1639." Church History 26 (1957): 325-241.

B15 Hanley, Thomas O'Brien. Their Rights and Liberties; The
     Beginnings of Religious and Political Freedom in Maryland.
     Westminster: Newman Press, 1959.

B16   Huhner, Leo. The Struggle for Religious Liberty in North
      Carolina. Philadelphia: American Jewish Historical
      Society, n.d.

B17   Hurley, James M. "The Political Status of Roman Catholics
      in North Carolina." Records of the American Catholic
      Historical Society 38 (1927): 237-296.

B18   Ireland, O. S. "The Ethnic-Religious Dimension of
      Pennsylvania Politics, 1778-1779." William & Mary
      Quarterly 30 (1973): 423-448.

B19   Ives, J. Moss. "The Catholic Contribution to Religious
      Liberty in Colonial America." Catholic Historical
      Review 21 (1935): 283-298.

B20   Ives, J. Moss. The Ark and the Dove: The Beginning of
      Civil and Religious Liberties in America. New York:
      Longmans Green, 1936.

B21   James, Charles F. Documentary History of the Struggle
      for Religious Liberty in Virginia. Lynchburg, Virginia:
      J. P. Bell Co., 1900. (Reprint by Da Capo Press, 1971).

B22   Kennedy, William H. "Catholics in Massachusetts Before
      1750." Catholic Historical Review 17 (1931): 10-28.

B23   King, William. "Lord Baltimore and His Freedom in Granting
      Religious Toleration." American Catholic Historical
      Society of Philadelphia Records 32 (1921): 295-313.

B24   Kinney, Charles B. Church and State: The Struggle for
      Separation in New Hampshire, 1630-1900. New York:
      Teacher's College of Columbia University, 1955.

B25   Kite, St. Alban. "William Penn and the Catholic Church in
      America." Catholic Historical Review 13 (1927): 480-496.

B26   Lauer, Paul E. Church and State in New England. Baltimore:
      Johns Hopkins Press, 1892. (Reprint by New York: Johnson
      Reprint Corp., 1973).

B27   Little, Lewis Peyton. Imprisoned Preachers and Religious
      Liberty in Virginia. Lynchburg, Virginia: J. P. Bell Co.,
      1938.

B28   Lord, Robert H. "Religious Liberty in New England."
      Catholic Historical Records and Studies 22 (1932): 7-31.

B29   Malbin, Michael J. Religion and Politics: The Intentions
      of the Authors of the First Amendment. Washington:
      American Enterprise Institute, 1978.

B30 Marraro, Howard A. "Rome and the Catholic Church in the
     Eighteenth-Century Magazines." Catholic Historical
     Review 32 (1946): 157-189.

B31 Meyer, Jacob C. Church and State in Massachusetts, 1750-
     1833. Cleveland: Western Reserve University Press, 1930.
     (Reprint by New York: Russell & Russell, 1968).

B32 Moran, Denis M. "Anti-Catholicism in Early Maryland
     Politics." Records of the American Catholic Historical
     Society 61 (1950): 139-154, 213-256.

B33 Petrie, George. Church and State in Early Maryland.
     Baltimore: Johns Hopkins Press, 1892. (Reprint by
     New York: Johnson Reprint Corp., 1973).

B34 Ray, Mary Augustana. American Opinion of Roman Catholicism
     in the Eighteenth Century. New York: Columbia University
     Press, 1936.

B35 Readhead, Marjorie M. "Religious Intolerance in the
     Massachusetts Bay Colony." M.A. thesis. University of
     Detroit, 1932.

B36 Reed, Susan Martha. Church and State in Massachusetts,
     1691-1740. Urbana: University of Illinois, 1914.

B37 Riley, Arthur. Catholicism in New England in 1788.
     Washington: Catholic University of America Press, 1936.

B38 Spalding, Henry S. Catholic Colonial Maryland: A Sketch.
     Milwaukee: Bruce, 1931.

B39 Stille, Charles. "Religious Tests in Provincial Pennsylvania."
     Pennsylvania Magazine of History and Biography 9 (1888):
     365-406.

B40 Sweet, William Warren. "The American Colonial Environment
     and Religious Liberty." Church History 4 (1935): 43-56.

B41 Sweet, William Warren. "The Development of Religious Liberty
     in Colonial America." American Historical Review 40
     (1935): 435-445.

B42 Thom, William Taylor. The Struggle for Religious Freedom
     in Virginia: The Baptists. Baltimore: Johns Hopkins
     Press, 1900.

B43 Thorning, Francis Joseph. Religious Liberty in Transition:
     A Study of the Removal of Constitutional Limitations.
     Washington: Catholic University Press, 1931.

B44 Tillmanns, Walter G. "The First American Martyrs."
     Lutheran Standard 45 (November 2, 1965): 5-10.

B45 Weeks, Stephen Beauregard. Church and State in North
     Carolina. Baltimore: Johns Hopkins Press, 1893.
     (Reprint by New York: Johnson Reprint Corp., 1973).

B46 Winking, Lawrence H. "The Catholic Church in Congressional
     Debate, 1789-1827." M.A. thesis. Catholic University,
     1930.

SECTION C
THE ERA OF THE NATIVISTS AND KNOW-NOTHINGS
1830-1860

The first wave of religious prejudice, specifically aimed at Catholics, began in the 1840s when waves of Irish immigration lapped the U.S. shores. The so-called Native American or Nativist movement recruited allies from Protestants who were wary and suspicious of their historic rival.

The theological conflicts engendered soon moved to the political, educational and diplomatic sector. Violence erupted in several cities, including Philadelphia and New York. A convent in Massachusetts was burned to the ground. A priest was tarred and feathered in Maine. Dozens died in Philadelphia rioting caused by the issue of the Bible in the public schools. By the 1850s a full-scale political movement, called the "Know Nothings" capitalized on the religious conflict and threatened briefly to seize national power.

C12 remains the definitive work on this period. The bibliography in C12, as well as C13, includes many pamphlets and broadsides that reveal the flavor of that era. C6 is a colorful overview, while C56 mixes analysis with documentation.

Interpretive works that should be consulted include C2, C21, C27, C41, and C43.

Primary source documents include these books published by the Know Nothings themselves: C22, C54, C55, C64, C75. C18 was written by the prominent Catholic convert, Orestes Brownson, himself a political liberal and strong Democrat. His views are reflective of the Catholic elite during this trying time. C107 is a rare example of an anti-Protestant tirade that circulated among conservative Catholics.

Nativism's impact on education is discussed in C32, C35, C53, C65, C66, C74 and C83. The political battles are vividly depicted in C15, C17, C24, C36, C51, C57, C84 and C87. The dispute over American diplomatic relations with the Papal States is the focus for C33, C62, C88 and C99.

Most of the other works cited are regional portraits of religious strife during this era.

C1   Baker, Jean H. "Dark Lantern Crusade - An Analysis of the Know-Nothing Party in Maryland." M.A. thesis. Johns Hopkins University, 1965.

C2   Barry, Colman J. "Some Roots of American Nativism." Catholic Historical Review 44 (July, 1958): 137-146.

C3   Barry, John Paul. "Know-Nothing Party in the District of
      Columbia." M.A. thesis. Catholic University, 1933.

C4   Battersby, Sister Agnes C. "Public Opinion on the Syllabus
      Errorum of Pope Pius IX." M.A. thesis. Catholic
      University, 1953.

C5   Baughin, William A. "The Development of Nativism in
      Cincinnati." Bulletin of the Cincinnati Historical Society
      22 (October, 1964): 240-255.

C6   Beals, Carleton. Brass Knuckle Crusade. New York: Hastings
      House, 1960.

C7   Bean, William G. "An Aspect of Know-Nothings - The Immigrant
      and Slavery." South Atlantic Quarterly 23 (1924): 319-334.

C8   Bean, William G. "Puritan Versus Celt, 1850-1860." New
      England Quarterly 7 (1934): 70-89.

C9   Beckman, Robert E. "Louisville - Monday August 6, 1855."
      American Ecclesiastical Review 133 (October, 1955):
      239-252.

C10   Berger, Max. "The Irish Emigrant and American Nativism
      as Seen by British Visitors, 1836-1860." Pennsylvania
      Magazine of History and Biography 70 (1946): 146-160.

C11   Billington, Ray Allen. "Maria Monk and Her Influence."
      Catholic Historical Review 22 (1937): 283-296.

C12   Billington, Ray Allen. The Protestant Crusade, 1800-1860.
      New York: Rinehart, 1938.

C13   Billington, Ray Allen. "Tentative Bibliography of Anti-
      Catholic Propaganda in the United States, 1800-1860."
      Catholic Historical Review 18 (1933): 492-513.

C14   Bodo, John R. The Protestant Clergy and Public Issues,
      1812-1848. Princeton: Princeton University Press, 1954.

C15   Bowers, Douglas. "Ideology and Political Parties in
      Maryland, 1851-1856." Maryland Historical Magazine
      64 (Fall 1969): 197-217.

C16   Brand, Carl. "Know-Nothing Party in Indiana." Indiana
      Magazine of History XVIII (1922): 47+.

C17   Broussard, James H. "Some Determinants of Know-Nothing
      Electoral Strength in the South, 1856." Louisiana
      History 7 (Winter 1966): 5-20.

C18   Brownson, Orestes A.   "A Few Words on Native Americanism."
      Brownson's Quarterly Review 2 (Third Series) (July 1854):
      328-353.

C19   Buonocore, Sister M. Fabian.   "Political Nativism in
      Syracuse, New York." M.A. thesis. Catholic University
      of America, 1935.

C20   Bradley, Edward Scully. Henry Charles Lea: A Biography.
      Philadelphia: University of Pennsylvania, 1931.

C21   Carmen, Harry J. and H. Luthin Reinhard.   "Some Aspects
      of the Know-Nothing Movement Reconsidered." South
      Atlantic Quarterly 39 (194): 213-234.

C22   Carroll, Anna Ella. The Great American Battle or the
      Contest Between Christianity and Political Romanism.
      New York: 1856.

C23   Cole, Arthur C.   "Nativism in Lower Mississippi Valley."
      Proceedings of the Mississippi Valley Historical
      Association 6 (1912-1913): 258-275.

C24   Connors, Francis J.   "Samuel Finley Breese Morse and the
      Anti-Catholic Political Movement in the United States,
      1791-1872." Illinois Catholic Historical Review 12
      (1918): 83-122.

C25   Curran, Thomas J.   "Seward and the Know-Nothings." New
      York Historical Society Quarterly 51 (August 1967):
      140-159.

C26   Curran, Thomas J.   "Know-Nothings of New York State."
      Ph.D. dissertation. Columbia University, 1963.

C27   Davis, David Brion.   "Some Themes of Counter-Subversion:
      An Analysis of Anti-Masonic, Anti-Catholic, and Anti-
      Mormon Literature." Mississippi Valley Historical
      Review 47 (September, 1960): 205-224.

C28   Dehner, Sister M. Xavier.   "The Know-Nothing Party in
      Virginia, 1852-1860." M.A. thesis. Catholic University,
      1942.

C29   Desmond, Humphrey J. The History of the Know-Nothing Party.
      Washington: New Century Press, 1905.

C30   Deusner, C. E.   "The Know-Nothing Riots in Louisville."
      Register of the Kentucky Historical Society 6 (1943):
      122-147.

C31   Ernst, Robert.   "Economic Nativism in New York City During
      the 1840s." New York History 29 (1948): 170-186.

14   *Religious Conflict in America*

C32   Faherty, William B. "Nativism and Midwestern Education:
      The Experience of St. Louis University, 1832-1856."
      History of Education Quarterly 8 (Winter 1968): 447-458.

C33   Feiertag, Sister Loretta Clare. American Public Opinion
      on the Diplomatic Relations between the United States
      and the Papal States, 1847-1867. Washington: Catholic
      University Press, 1933.

C34   Feldberg, Michael. The Philadelphia Riots of 1844.
      Westport: Greenwood Press, 1975.

C35   Fell, Marie L. The Foundations of Nativism in American
      Text Books, 1783-1860. Washington: Catholic University,
      1933.

C36   Foik, Paul J. "Anti-Catholic Parties in American Politics,
      1776-1860." American Catholic Historical Society of
      Philadelphia Records 36 (March 1925): 41-69.

C37   Geffen, Elizabeth M. "Violence in Philadelphia in the
      1840s and 1850s." Pennsylvania History 36 (October
      1969): 380-410.

C38   Gohmann, Sister Mary de Lourdes. Political Nativism in
      Tennessee to 1860. Washington: Catholic University of
      America Press, 1938.

C39   Guerrieri, D. "Catholic Thought in the Age of Jackson,
      1830-1840: Equal Rights and Religious Freedom." Records
      of American Catholic Historical Society of Philadelphia
      73 (1962): 77-91.

C40   Haynes, G. H. "The Causes of the Know-Nothing Success in
      Massachusetts." American Historical Review 3 (1930):
      12-20.

C41   Higham, John. "Another Look at Nativism." American
      Catholic Historical Review 44 (July 1958): 147-158.

C42   Hinckley, Ted C. "American Anti-Catholicism During the
      Mexican War." Pacific Historical Review 31 (May 1962):
      121-137.

C43   Holt, Michael Fitzgibbon. "The Politics of Impatience:
      The Origins of Know-Nothingism." Journal of American
      History 60 (September 1973): 309-331.

C44   Horrocks, Thomas. "The Know-Nothings." American History
      17 (1983): 23-29.

C45   Hueston, R. F. "The Catholic Press and Nativism, 1840-1860."
      Ph.D. dissertation. University of Notre Dame, 1972.
      (Reprint by New York: Arno Press, 1976).

C46 Hurt, Peyton. "Rise and Fall of the Know-Nothings in
     California." Quarterly of the California Historical
     Society 4 (1930): 7-12.

C47 Keefe, Thomas M. "Chicago Flirtation with Political Nativism,
     1854-1856." Records 82 (1971): 131-158.

C48 Kenneally, J. J. "The Burning of the Ursuline Convent:
     A Different View." Records of American Catholic Historical
     Society, Philadelphia 90 (1979): 15-21.

C49 Kennedy, P. W. "The Know-Nothing Movement in Kentucky:
     Role of M. J. Spalding, Catholic Bishop of Louisville."
     Filson Club Historical Quarterly 38 (1964): 20-30.

C50 Koerber, Leonard G. "Anti-Catholic Agitation in Milwaukee,
     1834-1860." M.A. thesis. Marquette University, 1960.

C51 Koester, Leonard. "Louisville's 'Bloody Monday' - August 6,
     1855." Historical Bulletin 26 (1948): 53-54, 62-64.

C52 Kunth, P. F. "Nativism in California." M.A. thesis.
     University of California, 1947.

C53 Lannie, Vincent P. and Bernard C. Diethron. "For the Honor
     and Glory of God: The Philadelphia Bible Riots of 1844."
     History of Education Quarterly 8 (Spring 1968): 44-106.

C54 Laurens, J. Wayne. The Crisis: Or the Enemies of America
     Unmasked. Philadelphia: 1855.

C55 Lee, John Hancock. The Origin and Progress of the American
     Party in Politics. Philadelphia: 1855.

C56 Leonard, Ira M. and Robert D. Parmet. American Nativism,
     1830-1860. New York: Van Nostrand, 1971.

C57 Leonard, Ira M. "The Rise and Fall of the American Republican
     Party in New York City, 1843-1845." New York Historical
     Society Quarterly 50 (April 1966): 150-192.

C58 London, H. "The Irish and American Nativism in New York
     City, 1843-1847." Dublin Review 240 (1967): 378-394.

C59 Loyola, Sister. "Bishop Benedict J. Fenwick and Anti-
     Catholicism in New England, 1829-1845." United States
     Catholic Historical Society Records and Studies 27
     (1937): 99-256.

C60 Lucey, William. "Maine in 1854: Letters on State Politics
     and Know-Nothingism." American Catholic Historical
     Society of Philadelphia Records 65 (1954): 176-186.

C61   Lucey, William. "The Position of Catholics in Vermont:
      1853." American Catholic Historical Society of Philadelphia
      Records 64 (1953): 213-235.

C62   Marraro, Howard R. "The Closing of the American Diplomatic
      Mission to the Vatican and the Efforts to Revive It,
      1868-1870." Catholic Historical Review 33 (1948):
      423-447.

C63   Martin, Bernard Lee. "Cincinnati in 1853, a Study in
      Bigotry." M.A. thesis. Xavier University, 1950.

C64   Martin, Joseph H. The influence, Bearing and Effects of
      Romanism on the Civil and Religious Liberties of Our
      Country. New York: 1844.

C65   McCadden, J. J. "Bishop Hughes versus the Public School
      Society of New York." Catholic Historical Review 50
      (1964): 188-207.

C66   McCadden, J. M. "New York's School Crisis of 1840-1842:
      Its Irish Antecedents." Thought 41 (1966): 561-588.

C67   McConville, Sister St. Henry. Nativism in Pennsylvania.
      Washington: Catholic University Press, 1936.

C68   McConville, Sister St. Patrick. Political Nativism in
      the State of Maryland, 1830-1860. Washington: Catholic
      University of America Press, 1928.

C69   McEntry, Sister Blanche Marie. American Catholics in the
      War with Mexico. Washington: Catholic University Press,
      1937.

C70   McGann, A. G. Nativism in Kentucky to 1860. Washington:
      Catholic University of America Press, 1944.

C71   McGrath, Sister Paul of the Cross. Political Nativism in
      Texas, 1825-1860. Washington: Catholic University of
      America Press, 1930.

C72   McHugh, G. J. "Political Nativism in St. Louis, 1840-1857."
      M.A. thesis. St. Louis University, 1939.

C73   McSweeney, Edward F. "Judge William Gaston of North
      Carolina." United States Catholic Historical Society
      Records and Studies 17 (1926): 172-188.

C74   Meyers, M. A. "The Childrens' Crusade: Philadelphia
      Catholics and the Public Schools, 1840-1844." Records
      of American Catholic Historical Society, Philadelphia
      75 (1964): 103-127.

C75 Morse, Samuel F. B. The Imminent Dangers to the Free Institutions of the United States Through Foreign Immigration. New York: 1835.

C76 Mulkern, J. R. "The Know-Nothing Party in Massachusetts." Ph.D. dissertation. Boston University, 1963.

C77 Noonan, Carroll John. Nativism in Connecticut, 1829-1860. Washington: Catholic University Press, 1938.

C78 O'Driscoll, Sister M. Felicity. "Political Nativism in Buffalo, 1830-1860." American Catholic Historical Society of Philadelphia Records XLVII (1937): 279-318.

C79 Overdyke, W. D. The Know Nothing Party in the South. Baton Rouge: Louisiana State University Press, 1950.

C80 Parmet, Robert D. "Connecticut's Know-Nothings." The Connecticut Historical Society Bulletin 31 (July 1966): 84-90.

C81 Parmet, Robert D. "The Know-Nothings in Connecticut." Ph.D. dissertation. Columbia University, 1966.

C82 Pitt, Leonard. "The Beginnings of Nativism in California." Pacific Historical Review 30 (1961): 23-38.

C83 Pratt, J. W. "Religious Conflict in the Development of the New York City Public School System." History of Education Quarterly 5 (1965): 110-120.

C84 Purcell, Richard J. and John F. Poole. "Political Nativism in Brooklyn." The Journal of the Irish Historical Society 32 (1941): 10-56.

C85 Rand, Larry A. "The Know-Nothing Party in Rhode Island." Rhode Island History 23 (October 1964): 107-110.

C86 Ray, John M. "Anti-Catholicism and Know-Nothingism in Rhode Island." American Ecclesiastical Review 148 (January 1963): 27-36.

C87 Reinders, Robert C. "The Louisiana American Party and the Catholic Church." Mid-America 40 (1958): 218-228.

C88 Rush, Alfred C. "Diplomatic Relations: The United States and the Papal States." American Ecclesiastical Review 126 (1952): 12-27.

C89 Saint Henry, M. "Nativism in Pennsylvania with Particular Regard to Its Effect on Politics and Education, 1840-1860." Records of American Catholic Historical Society, Philadelphia 67 (1936): 5-47.

C90   Schafer, J. "Know-Nothingism in Wisconsin." Wisconsin
      Magazine of History 8 (1952): 3-21.

C91   Schmeckbier, Laurence Frederick. The Know-Nothing Party
      in Maryland. Baltimore: Johns Hopkins University Press,
      1899.

C92   Scisco, Louis D. Political Nativism in New York State.
      New York: Columbia University Press, 1901.

C93   Selig, Sister M. Lucy Josephine. "Know-Nothing Party in
      Florida, 1852-1860." M.A. thesis. Catholic University,
      1944.

C94   Senning, J. P. "The Know-Nothing Movement in Illinois."
      Journal Illinois State Historical Society 7 (1914-1915):
      9-29.

C95   Siracusa, Carl F. "Political Nativism in New York City,
      1843-1848." M.A. thesis. Columbia University, 1965.

C96   Soule, Leon C. The Know-Nothing Party in New Orleans.
      Baton Rouge: Louisiana State University Press, 1961.

C97   Stephenson, George M. "Nativism in the Forties and Fifties,
      with Special Reference to the Mississippi Valley."
      Mississippi Valley Historical Review 9 (1922): 185-202.

C98   Stickney, Charles. Know-Nothingism in Rhode Island.
      Providence: Rhode Island Historical Society, 1894.

C99   Stock, Leo F. United States Ministers to the Papal States,
      Instructions and Dispatches, 1848-1868. Washington:
      American Catholic Historical Association, 1933.

C100 Stritch, Alfred G. "Political Nativism in Cincinnati,
      1830-1860." American Catholic Historical Society of
      Philadelphia Records 48 (1937): 227-278.

C101 Thomas, Sister Evangeline. Nativism in the Old Northwest,
      1850-1860. Washington: Catholic University of America
      Press, 1936.

C102 Thompson, A. W. "Political Nativism in Florida." Journal
      of Southern History 15 (1949): 39-49.

C103 Thorp, Willard. "Catholic Novelists in Defense of Their
      Faith, 1829-1865." Proceedings of the American Antiquarian
      Society 78 (April 1968): 25-117.

C104 Treacy, Gerald C. "Father John Bapst, S. J. and the
      'Ellsworth Outrage.'" United States Catholic Historical
      Society Records and Studies 14 (1920): 7-19.

C105   Tuska, Benjamin.   "Know-Nothingism in Baltimore, 1854-1860."
       Catholic Historical Review 11 (1925): 217-251.

C106   Weinbaum, P. W.   "Temperance, Politics and the New York
       City Riots of 1857." New York Historical Society
       Quarterly 59 (1975): 246-270.

C107   Weninger, Francis X.   Protestantism and Infidelity.   New
       York: Sadlier & Co., 1864.

C108   William, Sister Charles A.   "The Know-Nothing Party in
       Missouri, 1855-1860." M.A. thesis. Catholic University,
       1945.

C109   Wooster, Ralph.   "An Analysis of the Texas Know-Nothings."
       Southwestern Historical Quarterly 70 (January 1967):
       414-423.

C110   Zwierlein, Frederick J.   "A Source of American No-Popery."
       St. Louis Fortnightly Review 40 (1933): 269-273.

SECTION D
THE ERA OF THE AMERICAN PROTECTIVE ASSOCIATION, 1870-1900

A new wave of Protestant-Catholic conflict began less than a decade after the war between the states. The question of state aid to parochial schools was a paramount one, though Protestants also expressed fears of increasing Catholic political influence in Washington.

Small-time groups like the Order of the American Union, and the National Committee to Preserve American Institutions were superceded by the American Protective Association, the most powerful anti-Catholic group of its time. It was also during this period that a book charging Catholics with the murder of Abraham Lincoln was circulated, (D21).

The chilling, apocalyptic nature of the rhetoric can be seen in D8, D18, D19, D34, D40, D50 and D56 - all primary works. The best study of the A.P.A. remains D30, though D14 and D57 are worth consulting. The parochial school aid question is tackled in D32. D48 is the best introduction to the earliest rumblings of controversy, while D49 should be read as the best underlying explanation for the persistence of anti-Catholicism during this half-century. Another thoughtful piece written during the conflict is D58.

One study (D4) deals with the Protestant-Reformist movement to "purify" American politics and government.

D1 Ander, Fritiof. "The Swedish American Press and the A.P.A."
    Church History 6 (1937): 173-177.

D2 Atchison, Carla Joan. "Nativism in Colorado Politics:
    The A.P.A. and the K.K.K." M.A. thesis. University
    of Colorado, 1972.

D3 Barnum, Samuel W. Romanism As It Is. Hartford: Connecticut
    Publishing Company, 1872.

D4 Blau, Joseph L. "The Christian Party in Politics." Review
    of Religion 11 (November 1946): 18-35.

D5 Brusher, J. S. "Peter Yorke and the A.P.A. in San Francisco."
    The Catholic Historical Review 37 (1951): 129-150.

D6 Burns, Allen W. "The A.P.A. and the Anti-Catholic Crusade,
    1885-1898." M.A. thesis. Columbia University, 1947.

D7 Chase, P. P. "Protestant Clergy in Massachusetts, 1884."
    Massachusetts Historical Society Proceedings 64 (1930-32):
    467.

D8   Christian, John T. America or Rome, Which? Louisville:
     1895.

D9   Clinch, B. J. "Anglo Saxonism and Catholic Progess."
     American Catholic Quarterly 25 (October 1900): 723-738.

D10 Considine, J. L. "Father Yorke: Champion of Human Rights."
     Ave Maria 31 (February 18, 1950): 200-208.

D11 Coudert, F. R. "The American Protective Association."
     Forum 17 (July 1894): 520-523.

D12 Coxe, Rt. Rev. A. Cleveland. Jesuit Party in American Politics:
     Letters to Monsignor Satolli. Boston: American Citizen Com-
     pany, 1894.

D13 Cross, Joseph L. "The American Protective Association:
     A Sociological Analysis of the Periodic Literature of
     the Period, 1890-1900." American Catholic Sociological
     Review 10 (1949): 172-187.

D14 Desmond, Humphrey J. The A.P.A. Movement. Washington, D.C.:
     New Century Press, 1912.

D15 Drury, A. W. "Romanism in the United States: The Proper
     Attitude Toward It." Quarterly Review of the United
     Brethren in Christ 5 (January 1894): 1-23.

D16 Froude, J. A. "Romanism and the Irish Race in the United
     States, Part I." North American Review 129 (1879): 519-536.

D17 Froude, J. A. "Romanism and the Irish Race in the United
     States, Part II." North American Review 130 (1880): 31-50.

D18 Fulton, Justin Dewey. Rome in America. New York: Funk
     and Wagnalls, 1887.

D19 Fulton, Justin Dewey. Washington in the Lap of Rome. Boston:
     W. Kellaway, 1888.

D20 Gladden, Washington. "The Anti-Catholic Crusade." Century
     47 (March 1894): 789-795.

D21 Harris, Thomas. Rome's Responsibility for the Assasination
     of Abraham Lincoln. Los Angeles: Heritage Manor, 1960.

D22 Herlihy, D. J. "Battle Against Bigotry: Father Yorke and
     the American Protective Association in San Francisco,
     1893-1897." Records of the American Catholic Historical
     Society of Philadelphia 62 (1951): 95-120.

D23 Higham, John. "The American Party, 1886-1891." Pacific
     Historical Review 19 (1955): 37-46.

D24   Higham, John. "The Mind of a Nativist: Henry F. Bowers
      and the A.P.A." American Quarterly 4 (1952): 16-24.

D25   Holmes, Byron Marshall. "The A.P.A. Movement." M.A. thesis.
      University of California, 1939.

D26   Hughey, George Washington. Political Romanism. New York:
      Carlton and Lanahan, 1872.

D27   Hynes, Sister Mary Callista. "The History of the A.P.A.
      in Minnesota." M.A. thesis. Catholic University of
      America, 1939.

D28   Johnson, Ross Seymour. "The A.P.A. in Ohio." M.A. thesis.
      Ohio State University, 1948.

D29   King, James M. Facing the Twentieth Century. New York:
      American Union League Society, 1899.

D30   Kinzer, Donald L. "Political Uses of Anti-Catholicism:
      Michigan and Wisconsin, 1890-1894." Michigan History
      39 (1955): 312-326.

D31   Omitted.

D32   Klinkhamer, Sister Marie. "The Blaine Amendment of 1875:
      Private Motives for Political Action." Catholic Historical
      Review 42 (1950): 15-49.

D33   Knuth, Priscilla Frances. "Nativism in California, 1886-
      1897." M.A. thesis. University of California, 1947.

D34   Lansing, Issac J. Romanism and the Republic. Boston:
      Arnold, 1890.

D35   Lathrop, George Parsons. "Hostility to Roman Catholics."
      North American Review CLIX (1894): 563-573.

D36   Lathrop, George Parsons. "Loyalty of Roman Catholics."
      North American Review CLIX (1894): 218-224.

D37   Lundvall, Howard Carl. "The A.P.A.: A Study of an Anti-
      Catholic Organization." M.A. thesis. University of
      Iowa, 1950.

D38   Mack, F. W. "Rum, Romanism and Rebellion." Harpers Weekly
      XLVIII (1904): 1140.

D39   Marsden, K. Gerald. "Father Marquette and the A.P.A.:
      An Incident in American Nativism." Catholic Historical
      Review 46 (1960): 1-21.

D40   McCallen, Robert S. Strangled Liberty, or Rome and Ruin.
      St. Louis: Columbia Book Concern, 1900.

D41   McFaul, James A. "Catholics and American Citizenship."
      North American Review 171 (September 1900): 320-332.

D42   McGlynn, Edward. "The New Know-Nothingism and the Old."
      North American Review 145 (August 1887): 192-205.

D43   Morton, Elizabeth. Rome and Washington. Chicago: Jones,
      1899.

D44   Murphy, Sister Mary Eunice. "The History of the A.P.A. in
      Ohio." M.A. thesis. Catholic University of America, 1939.

D45   Nary, R. "Church, State and Religious Liberty: View of the
      American Catholic Bishops of the 1890's." Ph.D. disser-
      tation. Georgetown University, 1967.

D46   "Papal Antichrist." Columbus Theological Magazine 12
      (August 1892): 239-244.

D47   Quirinus. "The Catholic Clergy in Politics." American
      Ecclesiastical Review 12 (January 1895): 44-50 and
      (March 1895): 218-226.

D48   Russ, William A. "Anti-Catholic Agitation during Recon-
      struction." Records of the American Catholic Historical
      Society 45 (1934): 312-321.

D49   Sewry, Charles. "The Alleged Un-Americanism of the Church
      as a Factor in Anti-Catholicism in the United States,
      1860-1914." Ph.D. dissertation. University of Minnesota,
      1955.

D50   Smith, Joseph Jackson. The Impending Conflict between
      Romanism and Protestantism in the United States. New York:
      E. Goodenough, 1871.

D51   Stauf, H. Margaret. "The Anti-Catholic Movement in Missouri:
      Post Civil War Period." M.A. thesis. Saint Louis
      University, 1936.

D52   Stough, Ruth Knox. "The A.P.A." M.A. thesis. University
      of Nebraska, 1931.

D53   Thomas, W. H. The Roman Catholic in American Politics.
      Boston: Albion, 1895.

D54   Traynor, W. J. H. "Policy and Power of the A.P.A." North
      American Review 162 (1896): 658-666.

D55   Traynor, W. J. H. "The Menace of Romanism." North American
      Review 161 (1895): 129-140.

D56   Van Dyke, Joseph S.   Popery, the Foe of the Church and of
      the Republic.   Philadelphia: People's Publishing Company,
      1871.

D57   Winston, Patrick Henry.   American Catholics and the A.P.A.
      Chicago: Charles H. Kerr, 1895.

D58   Wolff, G. D.   "Catholicism and Protestantism in Relation
      to our Future as a People."   American Catholic Quarterly
      Review 4 (January 1879): 159-163.

Addendum

D59   Menendez, Albert J.   "Why Did Mary Surratt Die?"   Liberty
      75 (September-October 1980): 22-23.

D60   Moore, Guy W.   The Case of Mrs. Surratt.   Norman: University
      of Oklahoma Press, 1954.

SECTION E
THE GUARDIANS OF LIBERTY, THE KU KLUX KLAN,
AND THE BIGOTED TWENTIES, 1900-1930

One of the most intense periods of religious conflict coincided with the increasing urbanization of our nation, and an enormous influx of immigrants from Eastern and Southern Europe in the decade preceding the Great War. The resulting cultural clash between the old Protestant culture and the rising tide of Catholicism and Judaism produced a backlash among Protestants.

Union Army General Nelson Miles and Georgia's demagogic Populist leader Tom Watson established a virulently anti-Catholic group called "The Guardians of Liberty" around 1910. Publishers brought out "The Menace," a large circulation weekly newspaper. The Railsplitter Press in Illinois poured forth a steady stream of propaganda aimed at averting the Roman Peril.

But the most serious threat was the revived Ku Klux Klan, which saw life once again on Stone Mountain, Georgia in 1915. It swept millions into its grip and nearly captured state governments in Oregon, Colorado, Indiana, Oklahoma and elsewhere. Because of its importance as a self-proclaimed defender of Anglo-Saxon Protestant values, the Klan deserved a special section. So I have separated material on the Klan into the latter portion of Section E.

Some good overviews of this entire era can be found in E13, E14, E19, and especially E23. Trenchant studies of the Catholic presence in America are to be found in E20 and E33. A sophisticated critique of Catholicism in E2 is answered effectively by a Catholic convert and one-time Episcopal bishop of Delaware in E27. E53 is a comprehensive review of anti-Catholicism by a noted Catholic intellectual.

For a biographical look at some of the colorful personalities attracted to the anti-Catholic crusade see E8 and E18.

Many renowned authors expressed themselves during this complicated and bigoted era: Hilaire Belloc (E3), Lloyd Douglas (E80), W. E. B. DuBois (E81) and George Santayana (E46).

Lurid examples of anti-Catholicism can be gleaned from E1, E6, E11, E34, E38, E41 and E50. An unusual suggestion that Protestantism was dying and Catholicism taking its place was advanced in E47.

Anti-Semitism is dealt with in E22, E15 and E29. An example of elitism aimed at all non-Anglo-Saxon Protestant groups is E17.

Several authors argue, with considerable documentation that the Klan represented conservative Protestant values and was closely related to fundamentalist clergy and churches throughout the country, including the Northern cities. The Klan fought for Prohibition, school prayer, Sunday closing laws, and censorship. See especially E92, E56-E59, E97, E91, E108, E75, E99, and E138. E110 tries unsuccessfully to exonerate the Protestant churches.

Students of this period should consult some of the writings of Klan supporters and leaders (E143, E146, E83-E86, E131) to see what motivated them. One Congregationalist minister (E98) thought the Klan wasn't so bad because the Catholics had the Knights of Columbus and the Jesuits! How a socially and politically distinguished Mississippi Catholic family reacted to the Klan can be seen in E120. Some of the Klan's horrors are depicted in E70, E123, E125, E113, and E60.

The Klan also sought to fire Catholic school teachers, firemen, policemen and government workers. See E121, E134, and E68.

E1 Autry, Allen Hill. **Warning Signals, or Romanism and American Peril.** Little Rock: 1911.

E2 Barrett, E. Boyd. **Rome Stoops to Conquer.** New York: Julian Messner, 1935.

E3 Belloc, Hilaire. "The Church and Anti-Catholic Culture." **Catholic World** 119 (September 1924): 742-745.

E4 Browne, P. W. "Lest We Forget." **Catholic World** 112 (December 1920): 331-340.

E5 Bucher, Betty R. "Catholics and Woodrow Wilson's Mexican Policy." M.A. thesis. Catholic University of America, 1954.

E6 Calloway, Timothy Walton. **Romanism vs. Americanism.** Atlanta: 1923.

E7 "Catholics and Prohibition." **Literary Digest** 65 (April 10, 1920): 44-45.

E8 Clark, William Lloyd. **The Story of My Battle with the Scarlet Beast.** Milan: Rail Splitter Press, 1932.

E9 Clark, William Lloyd. **Hell at Midnight in Springfield.** Milan: Truth and Light Publishing House, 1910.

E10 Conen, Cyril John. "Politico-Religious Disturbances in Indiana, 1922-1926." M.A. thesis. Catholic University, 1938.

E11 Crowley, Jeremiah J. Romanism: A Menace to the Nation. Aurora: The Menace Publishing Company, 1912.

E12 Cuddy, E. "Are the Bolsheviks any Worse than the Irish?: Ethnic-Religious Conflict in America During the 1920's." Eire/Ireland 11 (1976): 13-32.

E13 Curry, Lerond. Protestant-Catholic Relations in America. Lexington: University of Kentucky, 1972.

E14 Davis, Lawrence B. Immigrants, Baptists and the Protestant Mind in America. Urbana: University of Illinois, 1973.

E15 Dinnerstein, Leonard. The Leo Frank Case. New York: Columbia University Press, 1968.

E16 Duffy, F. P. "What do the Methodists Intend to do?" Catholic World 95 (August 1912): 663-376.

E17 Fairchild, Henry P. The Melting-Pot Mistake. Boston: Little Brown, 1926.

E18 Flynt, Wayne. Cracker Messiah: Governor Sydney J. Catts Of Florida. Baton Rouge: Louisiana State University Press, 1977.

E19 Garrett, James Leo. Baptists and Roman Catholicism. Nashville: Broadman, 1965.

E20 Garrison, Winfred Ernest. Catholicism and the American Mind. Chicago: Willett, Clark, and Colby, 1928.

E21 Gladden, Washington. "The Anti-Papal Panic." Harpers Weekly 59 (July 18, 1914): 55-56.

E22 Golden, Harry. A Little Girl is Dead. Cleveland: World Publishing Company, 1965.

E23 Higham, John. Strangers in the Land: Patterns of American Nativism, 1860-1925. New Brunswick: Rutgers University, 1965.

E24 "Is There a Roman Catholic Peril in America?" Current Literature 52 (May 1912): 558-560.

E25 Keeffe, Richard J. "Guardians of Liberty." Catholic World 95 (April 1912): 97-108.

E26   Keeffe, Richard J. "Virtue of Bigotry." Catholic World
      99 (September 1914): 737-747.

E27   Kinsman, Frederick J. Americanism and Catholicism. New York:
      Longmans-Green, 1924.

E28   LaFontaine, Charles V. "Sisters in Peril: A Challenge
      to Protestant-Roman Catholic Concord, 1908-1918." New
      York History 58 (1977): 440-470.

E29   Lee, Albert. Henry Ford and the Jews. New York: Stein and
      Day, 1980.

E30   Longaker, Richard Pancoast. "Anti-Catholicism in the United
      States, 1919-1929." M.A. thesis. University of Wisconsin,
      1950.

E31   Marty, Myron A. Lutherans and Roman Catholicism: The
      Changing Conflict, 1917-1963. Notre Dame: University
      of Notre Dame, 1968.

E32   McKim, Randolph H. Romanism in the Light of History.
      New York: Putnams, 1914.

E33   Moore, John H. Will America Become Catholic? New York:
      Harper, 1931.

E34   Morrison, Henry Clay. Romanism and Ruin. Louisville:
      Pentecostal Publishing Company, 1914.

E35   Morton, Frances T. The Roman Catholic Church and its
      Relation to the Federal Governemnt. Boston: R. G.
      Badger, 1909.

E36   Mulherin, Sister Mary Jeane. "The First Years of the
      Catholic Layman's Association of Georgia, 1916-1921."
      M.A. thesis. Catholic University, 1954.

E37   Mullen, Sister Francis Charles. "Catholic Attitudes
      Towards Woodrow Wilson." M.A. thesis. Boston College,
      1960.

E38   Nations, Gilbert O. Rome in Congress. Washington: The
      Protestant, 1925.

E39   O' Shea, J. J. "Periodicity of Anti-Catholic Calumnies."
      American Catholic Quarterly 35 (July 1910): 496-508.

E40   Page, David P. "Bishop Michael J. Curley and Anti-Catholic
      Nativism in Florida." Florida Historical Quarterly XLV
      (October 1966): 101-117.

E41   Pickett, Leander Lycurgus. Uncle Sam or the Pope, Which?
      Louisville: Pentecostal Publishers, 1916.

E42   Pienkos, Donald. "Politics, Relgion and Change in Polish
      Milwaukee, 1900-1930." Wisconsin Magazine of History
      61 (1978): 179-209.

E43   Rackleff, Robert B. "Anti-Catholicism and the Florida
      Legislature, 1911-1919." Florida Historical Quarterly
      XLVIII (October 1970): 352-365.

E44   Reid, R. "Intolerance of the South." Catholic World
      127 (June 1928): 281-287.

E45   Ryan, John A. "Enduring Anti-Catholic Tradition."
      Commonweal 9 (April 24, 1929): 719.

E46   Santayana, George. "Alleged Catholic Danger." New Republic
      5 (January 15, 1916): 269-271.

E47   Smyth, Newman. Passing Protestantism and Coming Catholicism.
      New York: Scribners, 1908.

E48   Sweeney, Charles P. "Bigotry in the South." Nation 111
      (November 24, 1920): 585-586.

E49   Sweeney, Charles P. "Bigotry Turns to Murder." Nation
      113 (August 31, 1921): 232-233.

E50   Tipple, Bertrand M. Alien Rome. Washington: Protestant
      Guards, 1924.

E51   Vivian, James F. "The Pan American Mass, 1909-1914: A
      Rejected Contribution to Thanksgiving Day." Church History
      51 (September 1982): 321-333.

E52   Walsh, J. J. "Keeping Up the Protestant Tradition."
      Catholic World 101 (June 1915): 321-330.

E53   Williams, Michael. The Shadow of the Pope. New York:
      Whittlesey House, 1932.

E54   Wiltbye, John. "The Murderers of Father Coyle." America
      25 (August 27, 1921): 444-446.

THE KU KLUX KLAN AND RELIGIOUS STRIFE, 1915-1930

E55   Abbey, Sue Wilson. "The Ku Klux Klan in Arizona, 1921-1925."
      Journal of Arizona History 14 (Spring 1973): 10-30.

E56   Alexander, Charles C.   Crusade for Conformity: Ku Klux
      Klan in Texas, 1920-1930.   Houston: Texas Gulf Coast
      Historical Association, 1962.

E57   Alexander, Charles C.   The Ku Klux Klan in the Southwest.
      Lexington: University of Kentucky Press, 1965.

E58   Alexander, Charles C.   "Secrecy Bids for Power: The Ku
      Klux Klan in Texas Politics in the 1960's."   Mid-America
      XLVI (January 1964): 3-28.

E59   Alexander, Charles C.   "White-Robed Reformers: The Ku Klux
      Klan Comes to Arkansas."   Arkansas Historical Quarterly
      XXII (Spring 1963): 8-23

E60   Angle, Paul M.   Bloody Williamson: A Chapter in American
      Lawlessness.   New York: Knopf, 1952.

E61   Avin, Benjamin H.   "The Ku Klux Klan, 1915-1925:   A Study
      in Religious Intolerance."   Ph.D. dissertation.   Georgetown
      University, 1952.

E62   Bentley, Max.   "The Ku Klux Klan in Indiana."   McClure's
      LVII (May 1924): 23-33.

E63   Bentley, Max.   "The Ku Klux Klan in Texas."   McClures's
      LVII (May 1924): 11-21.

E64   Bliven, Bruce.   "From the Oklahoma Front."   New Republic
      XXXVI (October 17, 1923): 202-205.

E65   Bohn, Frank.   "The Ku Klux Klan Interpreted."   American
      Journal of Sociology XXX (January 1925): 385-407.

E66   Boyd, Thomas.   "Defying the Klan."   Forum LXXVI (July 1926):
      48-56.

E67   Bradley, Laura.   "Protestant Churches and the Ku Klux Klan
      In Mississippi During the 1920's."   M.A. thesis.   Univer-
      sity of Mississippi, 1962.

E68   Brownell, Blaine A.   "Birmingham, Alabama: New South City
      in the 1920's."   Journal of Southern History XXXVIII
      (February 1972): 21-48.

E69   Cates, F. Mark.   "The Ku Klux Klan in Indiana Politics,
      1920-1925."   Ph.D. dissertation.   Indiana University, 1970.

E70   Chalmers, David M.   Hooded Americanism: The First Century
      of the Ku Klux Klan, 1865-1965.   Garden City: Doubleday,
      1965.

E71 Chalmers, David. "The Ku Klux Klan in Politics in the
     1920's." Mississippi Quarterly XVIII (Fall 1965): 234-247.

E72 Chalmers, David. "The Ku Klux Klan in the Sunshine State:
     The 1920's." Florida Historical Quarterly XLII (January
     1964): 209-215.

E73 Clark, Malcolm, Jr. "The Bigot Disclosed: 90 Years of
     Nativism." Oregon Historical Quarterly LXXV (June 1974):
     108-190.

E74 Cline, Leonard L. "In Darkest Louisiana." Nation CXVI
     (March 14, 1923): 292-293.

E75 Conroy, Thomas M. "The Ku Klux Klan and the American
     Clergy." American Ecclesiastical Review LXX (1924):
     47-58.

E76 Crowell, Chester T. "The Collapse of Constitutional Govern-
     ment." Independent CIX (December 9, 1922): 333-334, and
     CX (January 6, 1923): 8-9.

E77 Omitted.

E78 Davis, James H. "The Rise of the Ku Klux Klan in Colorado.
     1921-1925." M.A. thesis. University of Denver, 1963.

E79 Davis, John Augustus. "The Ku Klux Klan in Indiana, 1920-
     1930." Ph.D. dissertation. Northwestern University, 1966.

E80 Douglas, Lloyd C. "The Patriotism of Hatred." Christian
     Century XL (October 25, 1923): 1371-1374.

E81 DuBois, W. E. Burghardt. "The Shape of Fear." North American
     Review CCXXIII (June 1926): 291-304.

E82 Duffus, Robert L. "Ancestry and End of the Ku Klux Klan."
     World's Work XLVI (September 1923): 527-536.

E83 Evans, Hiram W. "The Ballots Behind the Ku Klux Klan."
     World's Work LV (January 1928): 243-252.

E84 Evans, Hiram W. "The Catholic Question as Viewed by the
     Ku Klux Klan." Current History XXVI (July 1927): 563-568.

E85 Evans, Hiram W. "The Klan: Defender of Americanism."
     Forum LXXIV (December 1925): 801-814.

E86 Evans, Hiram W. "The Klan's Fight for Americanism." North
     American Review CCXXIII (March 1926): 33-63.

E87 Frost, Stanley. The Challenge of the Klan. Indianapolis:
     Bobbs-Merrill, 1924.

E88   Frost, Stanley. "The Masked Politics of the Klan and How
      the Candidacy of Smith May be Affected." World's Work
      LV (February 1928): 399-407.

E89   Fry, George T. "The Decline of Bigotry in America." Current
      History, XXVIII (June 1928): 396-402.

E90   Fry, Henry P. The Modern Ku Klux Klan. Boston: Small,
      Maynard and Company, 1922.

E91   Gatewood, Willard B., Jr. "Politics and Piety in North
      Carolina: The Fundamentalist Crusade at High Tide, 1925-
      1927." North Carolina Historical Review XLII (July 1965):
      275-290.

E92   Goldberg, Robert Alan. Hooded Empire: The Ku Klux Klan
      in Colorado. Urbana: University of Illinois Press, 1981.

E93   Goldberg, Robert Alan. "The Ku Klux Klan in Madison, 1922-
      1927." Wisconsin Magazine of History 58 (Autumn 1974): 31-44.

E94   Greene, Ward. "Notes for a History of the Klan." American
      Mercury V (June 1925): 240-243.

E95   Harrell, Kenneth Earl. "The Ku Klux Klan in Louisiana,
      1920-1930." Ph.D. dissertation. Louisiana State University,
      1966.

E96   Jackson, Charles O. "William J. Simmons: A Career in Ku
      Kluxism." Georgia Historical Quarterly L (December 1966):
      351-365.

E97   Jackson, Kenneth T. The Ku Klux Klan in the City, 1915-1930.
      New York: Oxford University Press, 1967.

E98   Jefferson, Charles E. Five Present-Day Controversies.
      New York: Fleming H. Revell Company, 1924.

E99   Jenkins, William D. "The Ku Klux Klan in Youngstown, Ohio:
      Moral Reform in the Twenties." Historian 41 (1978): 76-93.

E100 Johnston, Frank, Jr. "Religious and Racial Prejudices in
      the United States." Current History XX (July 1924): 573-578.

E101 Jones, Lila L. "The Ku Klux Klan in Eastern Kansas During
      the 1920's." Emporia State Research Studies XXIII (Winter
      1975): 5-41.

E102 Loucks, Emerson H. The Ku Klux Klan in Pennsylvania: A
      Study in Nativism. New York: Telegraph Press, 1936.

E103 Marriner, Gerald Lynn. "Klan Politics in Colorado." Journal
      of the West 15 (1976): 76-101.

E104 McBee, William D. The Oklahoma Revolution. Oklahoma City:
      Modern Publishers, 1956.

E105 Mecklin, John M. The Ku Klux Klan: A Study of the American
      Mind. New York: Harcourt, Brace and Company, 1924.

E106 Mecklin, John M. "Ku Klux Klan and the Democratic Tradition."
      American Review II (May-June 1924): 241-251.

E107 Melching, Richard. "The Activities of the Ku Klux Klan
      in Anaheim, California, 1923-1925." Southern California
      Quarterly 56 (1974): 175-196.

E108 Mellett, Lowell. "Klan and Church." Atlantic CXXXII
      (November 1923): 586-592.

E109 "Mer Rouge Murders Unpunished." Literary Digest LXXVI
      (November 1923): 586-592.

E110 Miller, Robert M. "A Note on the Relationship Between the
      Protestant Churches and the Revived Ku Klux Klan."
      Journal of Southern History XXII (August 1956): 355-368.

E111 Moseley, Clement C. "The Political Influence of the Ku
      Klux Klan in Georgia, 1915-1925." Georgia Historical
      Quarterly 57 (Summer 1973): 235-255.

E112 Mugleston, William F. "Julian Harris, the Georgia Press,
      and the Ku Klux Klan." Georgia Historical Quarterly 59
      (Fall 1975): 284-295.

E113 "The Murders of Mer Rouge." Literary Digest 76 (January 13,
      1923): 10-12.

E114 Murphy, Paul L. "Sources and Nature of Intolerance in the
      1920's." Journal of American History 11 (June 1964): 60-76.

E115 Myers, William S. "Know Nothing and Ku Klux Klan." North
      American Review CCXIX (January 1924): 1-7.

E116 Neuringer, Sheldon. "Governor Walton's War on the Ku Klux
      Klan." Chronicles of Oklahoma 45 (1967): 153-179.

E117 Nicholson, Meredith. "Hoosier Letters and the Ku Klux."
      Bookman 67 (March 1928): 7-11.

E118 Papanikolas, Helen Z. "Tragedy and Hate." Utah Historical
      Quarterly 38 (Spring 1970): 176-181.

E119   Patton, R. A. "A Ku Klux Klan Reign of Terror." Current
       History 28 (April 1928) 51-55.

E120   Percy, William A. Lanterns on the Levee; Recollections of
       a Planter's Son. New York: Alfred A. Knopf, 1941.

E121   Racine, Philip N. "The Ku Klux Klan, Anti-Catholicism, and
       Atlanta's Board of Education, 1916-1927." Georgia
       Historical Quarterly 57 (Spring 1973): 63-75.

E122   Rambow, Charles. "The Ku Klux Klan in the 1920's" South
       Dakota History 4 (1973): 63-81.

E123   Randel, William P. The Ku Klux Klan: A Century of Infamy.
       Philadelphia: Chilton Books, 1965.

E124   Rice, Arnold S. The Ku Klux Klan in American Politics.
       Washington, D.C.: Public Affairs Press, 1962.

E125   Rogers, John. The Murders of Mer Rouge. St. Louis:
       Security Publishing Company, 1923.

E126   Scott, Martin J. "Catholics and the Ku Klux Klan." North
       American Review 223 (June 1926): 268-281.

E127   Shankman, Arnold. "Julian Harris and the Ku Klux Klan."
       Mississippi Quarterly 28 (Spring 1975): 147-169.

E128   Shay, Frank. Judge Lynch; His First Hundred Years. New
       York: Washburn, 1938.

E129   Shumaker, W. A. "The Ku Klux Klan in Court." Law Notes
       27 (March 1924): 225-227.

E130   Silverman, Joseph. "The Ku Klux Klan a Paradox." North
       American Review 223 (June 1926): 282-291.

E131   Simmons, William J. America's Menace, or The Enemy Within.
       Atlanta: Bureau of Patriotic Books, 1926.

E132   Sloan, Charles W., Jr. "Kansas Battles the Invisible Empire:
       The Legal Ouster of the KKK from Kansas, 1922-1927."
       Kansas Historical Quarterly 40 (Autumn 1974): 393-409.

E133   Smith, Norman. "The Ku Klux Klan in Rhode Island." Rhode
       Island History 37 (May 1978): 35-45.

E134   Snell, William R. "Fiery Crosses in the Roaring Twenties:
       Activities of the Revived Klan in Alabama, 1915-1930."
       Alabama Review 23 (1970): 256-276.

E135   Stockbridge, Frank P.   "The Ku Klux Klan Revival."   Current
       History 14 (April 1921): 19-25.

E136   Sweeney, Charles P.   "The Great Bigotry Merger."   Nation
       115 (July 5, 1922): 8-10.

E137   Thornton, J. Mills, III.   "Alabama Politics, J. Thomas Heflin,
       and the Expulsion Movement of 1929."   Alabama Review XXI
       (April 1968): 83-112.

E138   Toll, William.   "Progress and Piety: The Ku Klux Klan and
       Social Change in Tillamook, Oregon."   Pacific Northwest
       Quarterly LXIX (April 1978): 75-85.

E139   Toy, Eckard V., Jr.   "The Ku Klux Klan in Tillamook, Oregon."
       Pacific Northwest Quarterly LIII (April 1962): 60-64.

E140   Tucker, Howard A.   A History of Governor Walton's War on
       Ku Klux Klan; The Invisible Empire.   Oklahoma City:
       Southwest Publishing Company, 1923.

E141   Turnbull, George S.   An Oregon Crusader.   Portland: Binfords
       & Mort, Publishers, 1955.

E142   Weaver, Norman F.   "The Knights of the Ku Klux Klan in
       Wisconsin, Indiana, Ohio and Michigan."   Ph.D. dissertation.
       University of Wisconsin, 1954.

E143   White, Bishop Alma.   Heroes of the Fiery Cross.   Zarephath:
       Good Citizen, 1928.

E144   Wieck, Agnes.   "Ku Kluxing in the Miners' Country."   New
       Republic XXXVIII (March 26, 1924): 122-124.

E145   Wilson, William E.   "That Long, Hot Summer in Indiana."
       American Heritage, XVI (August 1965): 56-64.

E146   Winter, Paul M.   What Price Tolerance.   New York: All-American
       Book, Lecture and Research Bureau, 1928.

For additional material on the Klan see William H. Fisher's

The Invisible Empire: a Bibliography of the Ku Klux Klan.

Metuchen: The Scarecrow Press, 1980.

SECTION F
RELIGIOUS CONFLICT, 1935-1965

World Wars and Depressions tend to mitigate religious conflicts, since people tend to see even their critics as fellow sufferers. This was true in the United States, though there was an upsurge of anti-Semitism in the late 1930s.

When peace and prosperity returned, however, the old Protestant-Catholic conflicts were reawakened. This time, the confident aggressiveness of the Roman Catholic Church has been seen by many observers as a contributory factor in post World War II religious antagonisms. Catholic positions on such issues as birth control, abortion and public aid to parochial schools contributed to Protestant fears and suspicions that American culture was being reshaped in a Catholic direction. Protestants also feared a loss of their religious liberty if Catholicism became dominant. All of these tensions culminated in the Presidential campaign of John F. Kennedy in 1960. (See Section J)

Catholics who acknowledged their church's responsibility for interfaith tensions were numerous. See F57, F25, F64, F15, F47 and F65.

The classic critique of Catholicism's rising political and cultural power is, of course, F6. Similar liberal views can be found in F23 and F45. Other hard-hitting Protestant analyses can be gleaned from F13, F30, F35 and F50. Some Catholics rejected any responsibility for poor interfaith relations. (See F38, F16, F32). Some of the most fair-minded scholarship may be seen in F5, F7, F8, F21, F39, F48, F51, F54, and F63.

The tendency of many conservative Protestants to support right-wing extremist movements is documented in F11, F42, F44, F46, F53, F55, F61, and F62.

For material on the Coughlinite movement see F49 and F59. The religious conflicts engendered by the Spanish Civil War are explored in F9 and F12. Three views of anti-Semitism are found in F17, F29 and F56. The classic conflict over President Truman's attempt to establish diplomatic relations with the Vatican in 1951 is explored by F20, F27 and F39. A violently anti-Catholic diatribe, published by a well-known ex-priest near the end of this historical period, is F33. An unusual examination of anti-Protestant prejudice is found in F34 by a sociologist who claimed, "There is no real discussion of anti-Protestantism in the literature of social science."

F1   Anderson, Elin. We Americans: A Study of Cleavage in
     an American City. Cambridge: Harvard University Press, 1937.

F2   Bechtel, William R. "Protestants and Catholics." New
     Republic 128 (July 27, 1953): 11-12.

F3   "Bias: Anti-Catholic Bias in a Month's Reading of the
     U.S. Press." Time 31 (May 2, 1938): 49.

F4   Birdwhistell, Ira V. "Southern Baptist Perceptions of
     and Responses to Roman Catholicism, 1917-1972." Ph.D.
     dissertation. Southern Baptist Theological Seminary,
     1975.

F5   Bishop, L. K. "Catholic-Protestant Relations in the
     United States." Journal of Human Relations 9 (1960):
     29-47.

F6   Blanshard, Paul. American Freedom and Catholic Power.
     Boston: Beacon, 1949.

F7   Blum, Barbara and John J. Mann. "The Effect of Religious
     Membership on Religious Prejudice." Journal of Social
     Psychology 52 (August 1960): 97-101.

F8   Bowie, Walter Russell. "Protestant Concern Over Catholicism."
     American Mercury 69 (September 1949): 261-273.

F9   Crosby, Donald. "Boston's Catholics and the Spanish Civil
     War." New England Quarterly 44 (March 1971): 82-100.

F10 Crosby, Donald F. God, Church and Flag: Senator Joseph R.
     McCarthy and the Catholic Church, 1950-1957. Chapel Hill:
     University of North Carolina Press, 1978.

F11 Danzig, David. "The Radical Right and the Rise of the
     Fundamentalist Minority." Commentary 33 (April 1962):
     291-298.

F12 Darrow, R. M. "Catholic Political Power: A Study of the
     Activities of the American Catholic Church on Behalf of
     Franco During the Spanish Civil War, 1936-1939."
     Ph.D. dissertation. Columbia University, 1953.

F13 Elderkin, George W. The Roman Catholic Problem. New York:
     Vantage, 1954.

F14 Erskine, Hazel Gaudet. "The Polls: Religious Prejudice."
     Public Opinion Quarterly 29 (1965): 486-496.

F15 Fearon, John. "Tribal Feelings in Catholic Evaluations."
     Homiletic and Pastoral Review 54 (January 1954): 306-309.

F16 Gillis, James M. "Open Letter to Anti-Catholic Agitators."
     Catholic World 170 (March 1950): 406-412.

F17 Glock, Charles Y. and Rodney Stark. Christian Beliefs and
     Anti-Semitism. New York: Harper, 1966.

F18 Grant, Philip A. "Catholic Congressmen, Cardinal Spellman,
     Eleanor Roosevelt and the 1949-50 Federal Aid to Education
     Controversy." Records 90 (1979): 3-13.

F19 Gross, R. D. "Changing Image of Catholicism in America."
     Yale Review 48 (June 1959): 562-575.

F20 Hasting, Martin F. "United States - Vatican Relations."
     Ph.D. dissertation. University of California, 1952.

F21 Herberg, Will. "Sectarian Conflict Over Church and State."
     Commentary 14 (November 1952): 450-462.

F22 "Intolerance: Anti-Catholic Propaganda." Commonweal 42
     (July 13, 1945): 299.

F23 "Is There a Catholic Problem?" New Republic 97 (November 16,
     1938): 32-33.

F24 Jones, Ilion T. A Protestant Speaks His Mind. Philadelphia:
     Westminster, 1960.

F25 Kane, John J. "Catholic Separatism." Commonweal 58
     (June 26, 1953): 293-296.

F26 Kane, John J. "Protestant-Catholic Tensions." American
     Sociological Review 16 (October 1951): 663-672.

F27 Karmarkovic, Alex. "The Myron C. Taylor Appointment."
     Ph.D. dissertation. University of Minnesota, 1967.

F28 Lachman, Seymour P. "The Cardinal, the Congressman and
     the First Lady." Journal of Church and State 7 (Winter
     1965): 35-66.

F29 Livingston, Sigmund. Must Men Hate? New York: Harper
     and Brothers, 1944.

F30 Lowell, C. Stanley. "If America Becomes 51% Catholic."
     Christianity Today 3 (October 27, 1958): 8-12.

F31 Maranell, Gary M. "An Examination of Some Religious and
     Political Attitude Correlates of Bigotry." Social Forces
     45 (March 1967): 356-362.

F32 Martindale, C. C. "Are There Any More Bigots?" Catholic
     World 135 (April 1932): 1-8.

F33 McLoughlin, Emmet. Crime and Immorality in the Catholic
     Church. New York: Lyle Stuart, 1962

F34 Means, Richard L. "Anti-Protestant Prejudice." The Christian
     Century 78 (August 16, 1961): 979-980.

F35 Morrison, Charles Clayton. "Roman Catholicism and Protestantism."
     Christian Century 63 (May 8, 1946): 585-588, and (May 15,
     1946): 618-621.

F36 Niebuhr, Reinhold. "Whosoever Thou Art: Acrimonious
     Relations Between Catholics and Protestants." Time 50
     (September 29, 1947): 55-56.

F37 "One Holy Catholic Church; Anti-Catholic Politics."
     Commonweal 15 (January 6, 1932): 253-254.

F38 O'Neill, James M. Catholicism and American Freedom. New
     York: Harper, 1952.

F39 O'Brien, F. William. "General Clark's Nomination as
     Ambassador to the Vatican: American Reaction." Catholic
     Historical Review 45 (January 1959): 421-429.

F40 Pelikan, Jaroslav. The Riddle of Roman Catholicism. Nashville:
     Abingdon, 1959.

F41 "Protestants vs. Catholics." Time 47 (April 8, 1946): 68-69.

F42 Redekop, John Harold. The American Far Right: A Case
     Study of Billy James Hargis and Christian Crusade. Grand
     Rapids: Eerdmans, 1968.

F43 Reid, R. "Blue-Penciling the Editors; Anti-Catholicism in
     Georgia." Commonweal 22 (July 12, 1935): 279-281.

F44 Ribuffo, Leo P. The Old Christian Right: The Protestant
     Far Right From the Great Depression to the Cold War.
     Philadelphia: Temple University Press, 1983.

F45 "Roman Catholic Church Enters Politics." New Republic
     87 (July 8, 1936): 265-266.

F46 Roy, Ralph Lord. Apostles of Discord. Boston: Beacon, 1953.

F47 Scharper, Philip. "Why Protestants Fear Us." Ave Maria
     91 (May 28, 1960): 5-8.

F48 Sheerin, John B. "Protestant-Catholic Cold War." Catholic
     World 182 (December 1955): 161-165.

F49 Shenton, James P. "The Coughlin Movement and the New Deal."
     Political Science Quarterly 73 (1958): 352-373.

F50   "Should Protestantism Be Catholic-Conscious?"   Christian
      Century 54 (May 26, 1937): 670-672.

F51   Smith, Alston J.   "Catholic-Protestant Feud."   American
      Mercury 65 (November 1947): 536-542.

F52   Smylie, James Hutchinson.   "Catholics as Immigrants."
      Christian Century 80 (1963): 1396-1399.

F53   Smylie, James Hutchinson.   "Phases in Protestant-Roman
      Catholic Relations in the United States."   Religion in
      Life 34 (1965): 258-269.

F54   Sockman, Ralph W.   "Catholics and Protestants."   Christian
      Century 62 (May 2, 1945): 545-547.

F55   Stark, Rodney.   "Through a Stained Glass Darkly: Reciprocal
      Protestant-Catholic Images in America."   Sociological
      Analysis 25 (1964): 159-166.

F56   Strong, Donald S.   Organized Anti-Semitism in America.
      Washington: American Council on Public Affairs, 1941.

F57   Sugrue, Thomas.   A Catholic Speaks his Mind on America's
      Religious Conflict.   New York: Harper, 1952.

F58   Trese, Leo J.   "On Prejudice."   Commonweal 44 (May 17, 1946):
      125-126.

F59   Tull, Charles J.   Father Coughlin and the New Deal.
      Syracuse: Syracuse University Press, 1965.

F60   "Unbrotherly Division: Roman Catholics and Protestants in
      the U.S."   Time 46 (November 5, 1945): 61.

F61   Vinz, Warren L.   "The Politics of Protestant Fundamentalism
      in the 1950s and 1960s."   Journal of Church and State
      14 (Spring 1972): 236-260.

F62   Westin, Alan F.   "The John Birch Society: Fundamentalism
      of the Right."   Commentary 32 (August 1961): 93-104.

F63   Williams, G. H.   "Issues Between Catholics and Protestants
      at Mid-Century."   Religion in Life 23 (November 1954):
      176-181.

F64   Zahn, Gordon C.   "Catholic Separatism and Anti-Catholic
      Tensions."   America 96 (October 27, 1956): 94-98.

F65   Zahn Gordon C.   "The Content of Protestant Tensions:
      Fears of Catholic Aims and Methods."   American Catholic
      Sociological Review 18 (1957): 205-212.

Addendum

F66   Brown, Robert McAfee.   "Types of Anti-Catholicism."
      Commonweal 62 (November 25, 1955): 193-196.

F67   Deaton, Dorsey M.   "The Protestant Crisis: Truman's Vatican
      Ambassador Crisis of 1951."   Ph.D. dissertation.   Emory
      University, 1969.

F68   Garrett, James Leo, Jr.   "Protestant Writings on Roman
      Catholicism Between Vatican Council I and Vatican Council II."
      Ph.D. dissertation.   Harvard University, 1966.

SECTION G
RELIGIOUS CONFLICT, 1966-1984

The ecumenical euphoria of the mid and late 1960s seemed to herald a decline in religious conflict. And while overt hostility and deep-seated prejudice have declined, several public issues have reignited old hostilities.

In particular, the abortion controversy seemed likely to reawaken anti-Catholicism, producing what _Time_ called "an ecumenical war" (G5). The founding of the Catholic League for Religious and Civil Rights in 1973 symbolized fears among some Catholics that bigotry was making a comeback. (See G4, G7, G8, G9, G16, G24.)

Liberal supporters of freedom of choice on abortion attacked the Catholic Church as the main enemy (G27, G10, G15, G25). A series of articles by Dr. Stephen Mumford (G17-G21) brought the issue to the fore. Conservative Catholics cried foul (G11, G30, G32). They were in turn criticized by G33 and G23 and defended in G14 and G23 by non-Catholics.

At least three Protestant conservatives (G2, G13, G22) have decried the trends toward liberalism and ecumenism, feeling that Protestantism is the ultimate loser.

The involvement of liberal religionists, especially the National Council of Churches, in political activity came in for investigation (G1) and criticism (G31 and G34).

Three dispassionate analyses of religion and the abortion question in politics are to be found in G27, G28 and G35.

The persistence of anti-Semitism is probed in G3, G12 and G26.

G1   Adams, James L. _The Growing Church Lobby in Washington._ Grand Rapids: Eerdmans, 1970.

G2   Brown, Harold O. J. _The Protest of a Troubled Protestant._ New Rochelle: Arlington House, 1968.

G3   Dobkowski, Michael N. "American Anti-Semitism: A Reinterpretation." _American Quarterly_ 29 (Summer 1977): 166-181.

G4   "Do Catholics Have Constitutional Rights?" _Commonweal_ 105 (December 8, 1978): 771-773.

G5   "Ecumenical War over Abortion." _Time_ 113 (January 15, 1979): 62-63.

G6   Greeley, Andrew M. Ethnicity, Denomination and Inequality.
      Beverly Hills: Sage Publications, Inc., 1976.

G7   Greeley, Andrew M. An Ugly Little Secret: Anti-Catholicism
      in North America. Kansas City: Sheed, Andrews and McMeel,
      1977.

G8   Hitchcock, James. "Bigotry in the Press: The Example of
      Newsweek." The Alternative (now The American Spectator)
      3 (October 1976): 19-21.

G9   Hitchcock, James. On the Present Position of Catholics in
      America. New York: The National Committee of Catholic
      Laymen, 1978.

G10   Lader, Lawrence. Abortion II: Making the Revolution.
      Boston: Beacon Press, 1973.

G11   Largess, Robert P. Keeping Catholics in Their Place.
      Milwaukee: Catholic League for Religious and Civil Rights,
      1983.

G12   Lotz, Roy. "Another Look at the Orthodoxy - Antisemitism
      Nexus." Review of Religious Research 18 (Winter 1977):
      126-133.

G13   Lowell, C. Stanley. The Ecumenical Mirage. Grand Rapids:
      Baker Book House, 1967.

G14   Menendez, Albert J. "Anti-Catholicism Rears Its Ugly Head."
      New Oxford Review 47 (March 1980): 15-19.

G15   Merton, Andrew H. Enemies of Choice: The Right-To-Life
      Movement and Its Threat to Abortion. Boston: Beacon
      Press, 1981.

G16   Miller, Norman C. "A New Anti-Catholic Bigotry?" Wall
      Street Journal (December 14, 1978).

G17   "The Mumford Affair." The Humanist 43 (November/December
      1983): 5-10.

G18   Mumford, Stephen D. "Abortion: A National Security Issue."
      The Humanist 42 (September/October 1982): 5-10.

G19   Mumford, Stephen D. "The Catholic Church and Social Justice
      Issues." The Humanist 43 (July/August 1983): 5-14.

G20   Mumford, Stephen D. "Illegal Immigration, National Security
      and the Church." The Humanist 41 (November/December 1981):
      20-26.

G21 Mumford, Stephen D. "The Vatican and Population Growth
     Control: Why an American Confrontation?" The Humanist
     43 (September/October 1983): 18-24.

G22 Murch, James DeForest. The Protestant Revolt. Arlington:
     Crestwood Books, 1967.

G23 Nathanson, Bernard N. Aborting America. New York:
     Doubleday, 1979.

G24 Nauer, Barbara. "Catholic Academics and Secular Power."
     Homiletic and Pastoral Review 51 (May 1976): 53-63.

G25 Paige, Connie. The Right to Lifers. New York: Summit
     Books, 1983.

G26 Quinley, Harold E. and Charles Y. Glock. Anti-Semitism in
     America. New York: Free Press, 1979.

G27 Richardson, James T. and Sandie Wightman Fox. "Religion and
     Voting on Abortion Reform: A Follow-Up Study." Journal
     for the Scientific Study of Religion 14 (June 1975): 159-164.

G28 Richardson, James T. and Sandie Wightman Fox. "Religious
     Affiliation as a Predictor of Voting Behavior on Abortion
     Reform Legislation." Journal for the Scientific Study
     of Religion 11 (December 1972): 347-359.

G29 Sanders, Marion. "The Enemies of Abortion." Harper's
     248 (March 1974): 26-30.

G30 Schwartz, Michael C. "Bringing the Sexual Revolution
     Home: Planned Parenthood's Five-Year Plan." America
     139 (February 18, 1978): 114-116.

G31 Singer, C. Gregg. The Unholy Alliance. New Rochelle:
     Arlington House, 1975.

G32 Sobran, M. J. "Abortion as a Class Religion." National
     Review 22 (January 23, 1976): 28-31.

G33 Swomley, John M. "The Catholic League: Civil Rights or
     Sectarian Pressure?" Church and State 33 (October 1980):
     14-17.

G34 Time for Candor: Mainline Churches and Radical Social
     Witness. Washington: The Institute on Religion and
     Democracy, 1983.

G35 Vinovskis, Maris A. "The Politics of Abortion in the House
     of Representatives in 1976." Michigan Law Review 77
     (August 1979): 1790-1827.

SECTION H
RELIGIOUS CONFLICT AND PRESIDENTIAL POLITICS:
GENERAL STUDIES AND TITLES DEALING WITH ALL ELECTIONS EXCEPT
1928, 1960, 1976, and 1980

Religion - generally religious prejudice and hysteria -
has played a role in U.S. Presidential elections from the first
campaign of Thomas Jefferson to the victory of Ronald Reagan.
Its importance has varied from election to election. Religious
factors have been seen as crucial to the results in four elections
(1928, 1960, 1970, 1980). For this reason I have included a
separate section for each. (H, I, J and Q)

This section includes overviews of religion in politics.
(H19, H63, H65, H68, H85), studies of certain religious groups
(H39, H16, H22, H24, H25, H41, H93) and particularly significant
writings about elections other than the four previously mentioned.
(H42, H49, H18, H40)

Certain books and articles are indispensable. They include
H16, H49, H50, H73, H75, H32, H33, H59, H71, H5, H37, H64, H86.

H1   Allen, Lee N. "The Democratic Presidential Primary Election
     of 1924 in Texas." Southwestern Historical Quarterly LXI
     (April 1958): 474-493.

H2   Allen, Lee N. "The McAdoo Campaign for the Presidential
     Nomination in 1924." Journal of Southern History XXIX
     (May 1963): 211-228.

H3   Allinsmith, Wesley and Beverly. "Religious Affiliation and
     Politico-Economic Attitudes." Public Opinion Quarterly
     12 (1948): 377-389.

H4   Baum, D. "The 'Irish Vote' and Party Politics in Massachusetts,
     1860-1876." Civil War History 26 (1980): 117-141.

H5   Benson, Peter L. and Merton P. Strommen. Religion on Capitol
     Hill. San Francisco: Harper and Row, 1982.

H6   Blanshard, Paul. God and Man in Washington. Boston: Beacon,
     1960.

H7   Blum, Virgil C. Catholic Parents, Political Eunuchs. St. Cloud,
     Minnesota: North Star Press, 1972.

H8   Burchell, R. A. "Did the Irish and German Voters Desert the
     Democrats in 1920? A Tentative Statistical Answer."
     Journal of American Studies 6 (1972): 153-164.

H9   Byrne, Edward John. "The Religious Issue in National Politics."
     Catholic Historical Review 14 (June 1928): 329-369.

H10   Byrne, Edward John. "Anti-Catholicism in National Politics."
      M.A. thesis. Catholic University of America, 1928.

H11   Canavan, Francis. "Politics and Catholicism." Social Order
      9 (December 1959): 458-463.

H12   "Catholics, Non-Catholics, and Senator McCarthy." Commonweal
      59 (April 2, 1954): 639-640.

H13   "Changes in Attitudes Toward a Catholic for President."
      Journalism Quarterly 37 (Winter 1963): 12-20.

H14   Cuddy, E. "Irish-Americans and 1916 Election: An Episode
      in Immigrant Adjustment." American Quarterly 21 (1969):
      228-243.

H15   Cummings, S. "A Critical Examination of the Portrayal of
      Catholic Immigrants in American Political Life." Ethnicity
      6 (1979): 197-214.

H16   Dawidowicz, Lucy S. and Leon J. Goldstein. Politics in a
      Pluralist Democracy. New York: Institute of Human Relations
      Press, 1963.

H17   De Santis, Vincent P. "American Catholics and McCarthyism."
      Catholic Historical Review 51 (April 1965): 1-30.

H18   De Santis, Vincent P. "Catholicism and Presidential Elections,
      1865-1900." Mid-America 42 (April 1960): 67-79.

H19   Dulce, Berton and Edward J. Richter. Religion and the
      Presidency. New York: Macmillan, 1962.

H20   Farnham, Wallace D. "The Religious Issue in American Politics:
      An Historical Commentary." Queens Quarterly 68 (1961): 47-65.

H21   Fee, J. L. "Party Identification Among American Catholics,
      1972, 1973." Ethnicity 3 (1976): 53-69.

H22   Fenton, John. The Catholic Vote. New Orleans: Hauser, 1960.

H23   Fisher, Paul A. "The Catholic Vote - A Sleeping Giant."
      Triumph 9 (June 1974): 30-36.

H24   Flynn, George Q. American Catholics and the Roosevelt
      Presidency, 1932-1936. Lexington: University Press of
      Kentucky, 1968.

H25   Flynn, George Q. Roosevelt and Romanism: Catholics and
      American Diplomacy. Westport: Greenwood Press, 1976.

H26   Foik, Paul J. "Anti-Catholic Parties in American Politics,
      1776-1860." American Catholic Historical Society of
      Philadelphia Records 36 (1925): 41-69.

H27   Ford P. "The Irish Vote in the Pending Presidential
      Election." North American Review 147 (1888): 185-190.

H28   Frankovic, Kathleen. "The Influence of Religion on
      Political Behavior." Ph.D. dissertation. Rutgers
      University, 1974.

H29   Freeman, Donald McKinley. "Religion and Southern Politics:
      The Political Behavior of Southern White Protestants."
      Ph.D. Dissertation. University of North Carolina, 1964.

H30   Fuchs, Lawrence H. The Political Behavior of American Jews.
      New York: Free Press, 1956.

H31   Fuchs, Lawrence H. "Presidential Politics in Boston: The
      Irish Response to Stevenson." New England Quarterly
      30 (1957): 435-447.

H32   Fuchs, Lawrence H. "The Religious Vote." Catholic World
      200 (February 1965): 289-293.

H33   Fuchs, Lawrence H. "Religious Vote, Fact or Fiction?"
      Catholic World 192 (October 1960): 9-14.

H34   Glantz, Oscar. "Protestant and Catholic Voting in a
      Metropolitan Area." Public Opinion Quarterly 23 (Spring
      1959): 73-82.

H35   Gelman, Norman I. "Religion in Politics." Editorial Research
      Reports 2 (September 9, 1959): 673-694.

H36   Gold, David. "The Influence of Religious Affiliation on
      Voting Behavior." Ph.D. dissertation. University of
      Chicago, 1953.

H37   Grupp, F. W. "Political Ideology and Religious Preference:
      The John Birch Society and the A.P.A." Journal for the
      Scientific Study of Religion 12 (1973): 401-413.

H38   Hammond, John L. The Politics of Benevolence: Revival
      Religion and American Voting Behavior. Norwood, New Jersey:
      Ablex Publishing Corporation, 1979.

H39   Hanna, Mary. Catholics in American Politics. Cambridge:
      Harvard University Press, 1979.

H40   Hornig, Edgar A. "The Religious Issue in the Taft-Bryan
      Duel of 1908." Proceedings of the American Philosophical
      Society 105 (1961): 530-537.

H41   Isaacs, Stephen D. Jews and American Politics. New York:
      Doubleday, 1974.

H42   Jensen, Richard J. The Winning of the Midwest: Social and
      Political Conflict, 1888-1896. Chicago: University of
      Chicago Press, 1971.

H43   Johnson, Benton. "Ascetic Protestantism and Political
      Preference in the Deep South." American Journal of
      Sociology 69 (1964): 356-366.

H44   Johnson, Benton. "Ascetic Protestantism and Political
      Preference." Public Opinion Quarterly 2 (1962): 35-46.

H45   Johnson, Benton. "Theology and Party Preference Among
      Protestant Clergy." American Sociological Review 31
      (April 1966): 200-207.

H46   Jorstad, Erling. The Politics of Doomsday. Nashville:
      Abingdon Press, 1970.

H47   Kane, John J. "Catholic President?" Commonweal 63
      (February 17, 1956): 511-513.

H48   Karfunkel, Thomas and Thomas W. Ryley. The Jewish Seat:
      Anti-Semitism and the Appointment of Jews to the Supreme
      Court. Hicksville: Exposition Press, 1978.

H49   Kleppner, Paul. The Cross of Culture. New York: The Free
      Press, 1970.

H50   Kleppner, Paul. The Third Electoral System, 1853-1892.
      Chapel Hill: University of North Carolina Press, 1979.

H51   Knebel, Fletcher. "Can a Catholic Become Vice President?"
      Look 20 (June 12, 1956): 33-35.

H52   Kroke, David. "Religion, Stratification and Politics:
      America in the 1960s." American Journal of Political
      Science 18 (May 1974) 331-345.

H53   Lachman, Seymour P. "Barry Goldsmith and the 1964 Religious
      Issue." Journal of Church and State 10 (Autumn 1968): 389-404.

H54   Lapomarda, Vincent A. "A Jesuit Runs for Congress: The
      Rev. Robert F. Drinan and His 1970 Campaign." Journal of
      Church and State 15 (Spring 1973): 205-222.

H55   Leary, W. M., Jr. "Woodrow Wilson, Irish-Americans and the
      Elections of 1916." Journal of American History 54 (1967):
      57-72.

H56   Lipset, Seymour Martin. "Some Statistics on Bigotry in
      Voting." Commentary 30 (October 1960): 286-290.

H57   Lowell, C. Stanley. "Catholics, Protestants and Politics."
      Christianity Today 3 (July 20, 1959): 5-8.

H58 McAvoy, Thomas T. "Where is the Catholic Vote?" Ave Maria
     83 (June 16, 1956): 12-16.

H59 McCormick, Richard L. "Ethno-Cultural Interpretations of
     American Voting Behavior." Political Science Quarterly
     89 (June 1974): 351-377.

H60 McKinney, Madge W. "Religion and Elections." Public Opinion
     Quarterly 8 (Spring 1944).

H61 McManamin, Francis G. "American Bishops and the American
     Electorate." American Ecclesiastical Review 151 (1964):
     217-229.

H62 McWilliams, Carey. "The Church-State Issue." Nation 214
     (April 24, 1972): 515-516.

H63 Menendez, Albert J. Religion at the Polls. Philadelphia:
     Westminster Press, 1977.

H64 Miller, William Lee. "The Religious Revival and American
     Politics." Confluence 4 (1955): 44-56.

H65 Morgan, Richard E. The Politics of Religious Conflict.
     New York: Pegasus, 1968.

H66 Novak, Michael. "Can a Protestant be Nominated?" Christian
     Century 92 (July 9, 1975): 659-662.

H67 Novak, Michael. "Jewish Agenda, Catholic Agenda." Commonweal
     100 (June 28, 1974): 351, 367.

H68 Odegard, Peter H., ed. Religion and Politics. New York:
     Oceana, Dobbs Ferry, 1960.

H69 O'Grady, Joseph T. "The Roman Question in American Politics:
     1885." Journal of Church and State 10 (1968): 365-377.

H70 Orum, Anthony M. "Religion and the Rise of the Radical
     Whites: The Case of Southern Wallace Support in 1968."
     Social Science Quarterly 51 (December 1970): 674-688.

H71 Parenti, Michael. "Political Values and Religious Cultures:
     Jews, Catholics and Protestants." Journal for the Scientific
     Study of Religion 6 (Fall 1967): 259-269.

H72 Peden, J. R. "Charles O'Conor and the 1872 Presidential
     Election." The Recorder 37 (1976): 80-90.

H73 Pierard, Richard V. The Unequal Yoke. Philadelphia: J. B.
     Lippincott Company, 1970.

H74 Proof of Rome's Political Meddling in America. Washington:
     Fellowship Forum, 1927.

H75   Rischin, Moses.   Our Own Kind.   Santa Barbara: Center for the
      Study of Democratic Institutions, 1960.

H76   Roucek, Joseph S.   "American Ethnic and Religious Minorities
      in American Politics."   Politics 24 (1959): 84-100.

H77   Roucek, Joseph S.   "The Role of Religion in American Politics."
      Journal of Human Relations 11 (1963): 350-362.

H78   Rosen, Roberta.   "A Roman Catholic Runs for President: A
      Comparison of the Anti-Catholic Literature in the Nineteenth
      Century and in the Presidential Campaign of 1928 and 1960.
      M.A. thesis.   Smith College, 1961.

H79   Russell, C. Allyn.   "William Jennings Bryan, Statesman,
      Fundamentalist."   Journal of Presbyterian History 53
      (Summer 1975): 93-119.

H80   Shea, John Gilmary.   "The Anti-Catholic Issue in the Late
      Election - The Relation of Catholics to Political Parties."
      American Catholic Quarterly Review 6 (1881): 36-50.

H81   Sievers, Harry J.   "The Catholic Indian School Issue and
      the Presidential Election of 1892."   Catholic Historical
      Review 38 (July 1952): 129-155.

H82   Skillin, E.   "Catholic Press and the Election."   Commonweal
      33 (November 1, 1940): 50-52.

H83   Smith, M. S.   "The Influence of the Irish Vote in Chicago
      and the Elections of 1884, 1888, and 1892."   M.A. thesis.
      University of Notre Dame, 1958.

H84   Stauffer, A. P.   "Anti-Catholicism in American Politics,
      1865-1900."   Ph.D. dissertation.   Harvard University, 1933.

H85   Stedman, Murray S.   Religion and Politics in America.   New
      York: Harcourt, Brace and World, 1964.

H86   Stellway, R. J.   "The Correspondence Between Religious
      Orientation and Socio-Political Liberalism and Conservatism."
      Sociological Quarterly 14 (1973): 430-439.

H87   Streiker, Lowell D. and Gerald S. Strober.   Religion and the
      New Majority.   New York: Association Press, 1972.

H88   Sweeney, K.   "Rum, Romanism, Representatives and Reform:
      Coalition Politics in Massachusetts, 1847-1853."   Civil
      War History 22 (1976): 116-137.

H89   Swomley, John M.   "Manipulating the Blocs: Church, State
      and Mr. Nixon."   Nation 215 (September 11, 1972): 168-171.

H90 Teller, Judd L. "The Jewish Vote - Myth or Fact?" Midstream
     7 (Summer 1960): 4-8.

H91 Vinz, Warren. "Protestant Fundamentalism and McCarthy."
     Continuum 6 (Fall 1968): 314-325.

H92 Walker, Brooks R. The Christian Fright Peddlers. New York:
     Doubleday and Company, Inc., 1964.

H93 Weyl, Nathaniel. The Jew in American Politics. New Rochelle:
     Arlington House, 1968.

H94 Wyman, Robert E. "Wisconsin Ethnic Groups and the Election
     of 1890." Wisconsin Magazine of History 51 (Summer 1968):
     269-290.

H95 Younger, George D. "Protestant Piety and the Right Wing."
     Social Action 17 (1951): 5-35.

SECTION I
THE AL SMITH CAMPAIGN, 1928

The defeat of Alfred E. Smith in 1928 was clearly due to religious prejudice. That is the indisputable conclusion of historian Allan J. Lichtman (I17), whose 1979 book is simply the last word on the subject. While some excellent prior books and articles have probed this election, no one can any longer dispute that conclusion.

Some good voting studies can be found in I4, I27, I31, I1, I36, I38.

Some exciting impressionistic views include I23, I33, I3, I5, I6, I11, I18. Some primary source documents attacking Smith are I24, I30, I19, I20, while some defended him (I15, I29). See Smith's own article (I32).

I1   Baggaley, Andrew R. "Religious Influences on Wisconsin Voting, 1928-1960." _American Political Science Review_ 56 (1962): 66-70.

I2   Bradford, Richard H. "Religion and Politics: Alfred E. Smith and the Election of 1928 in West Virginia." _West Virginia History_ 38 (1975): 213-21.

I3   Burner, David B. "The Brown Derby Campaign." _New York History_ 66 (1965): 356-380.

I4   Burner, David. _The Politics of Provincialism_. New York: Alfred A. Knopf, 1968.

I5   Carleton, William G. "The Popish Plot of 1928: Smith-Hoover Presidential Campaign." _Forum_ 112 (1949): 141-147.

I6   Carter, Paul A. "The Campaign of 1928 Re-examined: A Study in Political Folklore." _Wisconsin Magazine of History_ 46 (1963): 263-272.

I7   Carter, Paul A. "The Other Catholic Candidate: The 1928 Presidential Bid of Thomas J. Walsh." _Pacific Northwest Quarterly_ 55 (1964): 1-8.

I8   Casey, R. D. "The Scripps-Howard Newpapers in the 1928 Presidential Campaign." _Journalism Quarterly_ 7 (1930): 207-231.

I9   Dabney, Virginius. _Dry Messiah: The Life of Bishop Cannon_. New York: Knopf, 1949.

I10   DeLamy, Sister Mary Dolora. "The Religious Issue of the Campaign of 1928 as Reflected in the Wisconsin Press." M.A. thesis. Catholic University, 1949.

I11   Doherty, Herbert J., Jr.   "Florida and the Presidential
      Election of 1928."   Florida Historical Quarterly 26
      (1947): 174-186.

I12   Fischer, Sister Mary Alexandrine.   "Illinois Editorial
      Opinion on the Alfred E. Smith Campaign."   M.A. thesis.
      Catholic University, 1950.

I13   Hattery, John W.   "The Presidential Election Campaigns of
      1928 and 1960:   A Comparison of The Christian Century and
      America."   Journal of Church and State 9 (1967): 36-50.

I14   Hofstadter, Richard.   "Could a Protestant Have Beaten Hoover
      in 1928?"   Reporter 22 (1960): 31-33.

I15   Hyland, James A.   Rome and the White House.   New York:
      Devin-Adair, 1928.

I16   Kelley, D. B.   "Deep South Dilemma: The Mississippi Press
      in the Presidential Election of 1928."   Journal of
      Mississippi History 25 (1963): 63-92.

I17   Lichtman, Allan J.   Prejudice and the Old Politics: The
      Presidential Election of 1928.   Chapel Hill: University
      of North Carolina Press, 1979.

I18   Lisenby, William Foy.   "Brough, Baptists, and Bombast: The
      Election of 1928."   Arkansas Historical Quarterly 32 (1973):
      120-131.

I19   Marshall, Charles C.   "An Open Letter to the Honorable Alfred
      E. Smith."   Atlantic Monthly 139 (April 1927): 670-689.

I20   Marshall, Charles C.   Governor Smith's American Catholicism.
      New York: Dodd Mead, 1928.

I21   McClerren, Beryl F.   "The Southern Baptist State Newspapers
      and the Religious Issue During the Presidential Campaigns
      of 1928 and 1960."   Ph.D. dissertation.   Southern Illinois
      University, 1963.

I22   Miller, Robert Moats.   "A Footnote to the Role of the
      Protestant Churches in the Election of 1928."   Church
      History 25 (1956): 145-159.

I23   Moore, Edmund A.   A Catholic Runs for President.   New York:
      Ronald, 1956.

I24   Nations, Gilbert O.   The Political Career of Alfred E. Smith.
      Washington, D.C.: The Protestant, 1928.

I25   Neal, N. E.   "The Smith-Robinson Campaign of 1928."   Arkansas
      Historical Quarterly 19 (1960): 3-11.

I26 Ogburn, William F. and Nell Snow Talbot. "A Measurement of the Factors in the Presidential Election of 1928." Social Forces 8 (1929): 175-183.

I27 Peel, Roy Victor and Thomas C. Donnelly. The 1928 Campaign, an Analysis. New York: R. R. Smith, 1931. (Reprinted by New York: Arno, 1974).

I28 Peterson, P. L. "Stopping Al Smith: The 1928 Democratic Primary in South Dakota." South Dakota History 4 (1974): 439-454.

I29 Ryan, John A. "A Catholic View of the Election." Current History 29 (December 1928): 377-381.

I30 Schroeder, Theodore. Al Smith, the Pope and the Presidency. New York: 1928.

I31 Silva, Ruth C. Rum, Religion and Votes. University Park, Pennsylvania: Pennsylvania State University, 1962.

I32 Smith, Alfred E. "Patriot and Catholic." Atlantic Monthly 139 (May 1927): 721-728.

I33 Smith, Rembert Gilman. Politics in a Protestant Church. Atlanta: 1930.

I34 Smith, W. D. "Alfred E. Smith and John F. Kennedy: The Religious Issue During the Presidential Campaigns of 1928 and 1960." Ph.D. dissertation. Southern Illinois University, 1964.

I35 Smylie, James H. "The Roman Catholic Church, the State and Al Smith." Church History 29 (1960): 321-343.

I36 Stange, Douglas C. "Al Smith and the Republican Party at Prayer: The Lutheran Vote - 1928." Review of Politics 32 (1970): 347-364.

I37 Straton, H. H. and F. M. Szasz. "The Reverend John Roach Straton and the Presidential Campaign of 1928." New York State History 69 (1968): 200-217.

I38 Watson, Richard A. "Religion and Politics in Mid-America: Presidential Voting in Missouri, 1928 and 1960." Mid-continental American Studies Journal 5 (1964): 33-55.

I39 Weeks, O. Douglas. "The Election of 1928." Southwest Political and Social Science Quarterly 9 (1928): 337-348.

Addendum

I40 Heath, Donald Floyd. "The Presidential Campaign of 1928:
     Protestant Opposition to Alfred E. Smith as Reflected in
     Denominational Periodicals." Ph.D. dissertation.
     Vanderbilt University, 1973.

I41 Murray, Spencer C. "The Role of Major Tennessee Denominations
     in the 1928 Presidential Campaign of Alfred E. Smith."
     Ph.D. dissertation. Vanderbilt University, 1971.

SECTION J
THE JOHN F. KENNEDY CAMPAIGN, 1960

The election of John F. Kennedy as America's first and only
Roman Catholic President created panic and fear among many Protestants (J19, J2, J4, J6, J21, J29, J31, J40) and intense excite-
ment and interest among everyone else.

This campaign generated writings and personal involvement
by famous writers like James Michener, James Pike, John C. Bennett
and Rienhold Niebuhr.

All of these selections deal with the religious issue in
1960, but J4, J14, J16, J13 are especially useful post-mortems.
J12, J16 and J24 look beyond one campaign to examine the impact
of the Kennedy Presidency on interfaith relations.

J1   Baker, Robert A. "The Presidency and the Roman Catholic
       Church." Journal of Church and State 2 (November 1960):
       112-116.

J2   Barnhouse, Donald Grey. "The Peril Over the Presidency."
       Eternity XI (October 1960): 8-10.

J3   Barrett, Patricia. "Religion and the 1960 Presidential
       Election." Social Order 12 (June 1962): 267-285.

J4   Barrett, Patricia. Religious Liberty and the American
       Presidency. New York: Herder and Herder, 1963.

J5   Bennett, John C. "The Roman Catholic Issue Again."
       Christianity and Crisis 20 (September 19, 1960): 125-126.

J6   Bianchi, Eugene C. John XXIII and American Protestants.
       Washington: Corpus Books, 1968.

J7   Bonnell, John Sutherland. "Religion and the Presidency."
       Presbyterian Life 13 (March 1, 1960): 8-10.

J8   Brenner, Saul. "Patterns of Jewish-Catholic Democratic
       Voting and the 1960 Presidential Vote." Jewish Social
       Studies 25 (July 1964): 4-8.

J9   Burns, James MacGregor. "The Religious Issue." Progressive
       24 (November 1960): 21-22.

J10 Canavan, Francis. "Politics and Catholicism." Social Order
       9 (December 1959): 458-463.

J11 Cater, Douglas. "The Protestant Issue." Reporter 22
       (October 13, 1960): 30-32.

J12 "Church-State Legacy of JFK." Journal of Church and State
       6 (Winter 1964): 5-11.

J13   Connell, Francis J. "Now That the Election is Over."
      American Ecclesiastical Review 144 (January 1961): 1-13.

J14   Converse, Phillip E. Religion and Politics: The 1960
      Election. Ann Arbor: University of Michigan Survey
      Research Center, 1961.

J15   David, Paul T., ed. The Presidential Election and Transition,
      1960-1961. Washington: Brookings Institution, 1961.

J16   Fuchs, Lawrence H. John F. Kennedy and American Catholicism.
      New York: Meredith Press, 1967.

J17   Hardon, John A. "A Catholic in the White House." Homiletic
      and Pastoral Review 60 (September 1960): 1134-1140.

J18   Hertzberg, Arthur. "The Protestant Establishment, Catholic
      Dogma and the Presidency." Commentary 30 (October 1960):
      277-285.

J19   Hillis, Don W. If America Elects a Catholic President.
      Columbus: Dunham Publishing Company, 1960.

J20   Hoyt, Robert. "Kennedy, Catholicism and the Presidency."
      Jubilee 20 (December 1960): 13-15.

J21   Johnson, Howard. "Are American Catholics Different?"
      Watchman-Examiner XLVIII (September 1, 1960): 687-881.

J22   Kim, Richard C. C. "A Roman Catholic President in the
      American Schema." Journal of Church and State 3
      (May 1961): 33-40.

J23   Manz, James G. "The Religious Significance of the 1960
      Presidential Election." Lutheran Witness LXXIX (November
      29, 1960): 10.

J24   Menendez, Albert J. John F. Kennedy: Catholic and Humanist.
      Buffalo: Prometheus Books, 1979.

J25   Michener, James A. Report of the County Chairman. New York:
      Random House, 1961.

J26   Niebuhr, Reinhold. "Catholics and the Presidency." New
      Leader 43 (May 9, 1960): 3-4.

J27   Niebuhr, Reinhold. "The Religious Issue." New Leader 43
      (December 12, 1960): 3-4.

J28   "On Raising the Religious Issue: a Symposium." America
      103 (September 24, 1960): 702-709.

J29   Palmer, Gordon. "Religion and the United States Presidency."
      Watchman-Examiner XLVIII (September 15, 1960): 720-721.

J30   Pike, James A. A Roman Catholic in the White House. New
      York: Doubleday, 1960.

J31   Price, Sterling L. "The Catholic-Protestant Dilemma."
      Watchman-Examiner XLVIII (September 29, 1960): 762-764.

J32   "The Religious Issue in the Presidential Campaign." Facts
      4 (June-July 1960): 151-160.

J33   Roper, Elmo. "The Catholic Vote: A Second Look." Saturday
      Review 43 (November 5, 1960): 27, 53.

J34   Roper, Elmo. "The Myth of the Catholic Vote." Saturday
      Review 42 (October 31, 1959): 22.

J35   Shinn, Roger L. "What the Campaign Did to Religion."
      Christianity and Crisis 20 (November 14, 1960): 161-163.

J36   Simon, Paul. "Catholicism and the Elections." Commonweal
      72 (July 22, 1960): 375-377.

J37   Sterling, Claire. "The Vatican and Kennedy." Reporter
      22 (October 27, 1960): 26-27.

J38   Vorspan, Albert. "Jewish Voters and the Religious Issue."
      Jewish Frontier 27 (October 1960): 8-11.

J39   Wicklein, John. "Religious Issue Revisited." American
      Judaism   (April 1961): 6, 30-31.

J40   Wilcox, Jackson. "Religion and Your Vote." Watchman-Examiner
      XLVIII (May 5, 1960): 368-369.

J41   Woelfel, La Salle. "The Oldest American Prejudice." America
      103 (September 24, 1960): 697-699.

Jimmy Carter's out-of-nowhere victory in 1976 made the term "born again politics" a household phrase. His campaign - and the fears, expectations, and religious realignment that it inspired - provoked some thoughtful reexaminations of religion in politics.

The commentaries range from the enthusiastic (K7, K10, K15, K16, K17) to the sarcastic (K18) to the watchful and wary (K8, K9, K4, K13).

K1   Adams, James Luther.   "The Fundamentalist Far Right Rides Again." Humanist 36 (September-October 1976): 22-23.

K2   Baker, James T.   A Southern Baptist in the White House. Philadelphia: The Westminster Press, 1977.

K3   Birdwhistell, Ira V.   "Southern Baptists and Roman Catholics." Ecumenist 14 (May-June 1976): 49-51.

K4   Boyd, Forrest.   "Do We Really Want a Saint in the White House?" Moody Monthly 77 (September 1976): 21.

K5   "The Catholic Issues."   Commonweal 103 (August 27, 1976): 547-548.

K6   Evans, Al.   "Southern Jews, Baptists and Jimmy Carter." New York Times (October 20, 1976).

K7   Hefley, James.   The Church That Produced a President. New York: Wyden Books, 1977.

K8   Himmelfarb, Milton.   "Carter and the Jews." Commentary 62 (August 1976): 45-48.

K9   Hunt, Albert R.   "Carter and Catholics." Wall Street Journal (July 8, 1976).

K10 Kucharsky, David.   The Man from Plains. New York: Harper and Row, 1976.

K11 Menendez, Albert J.   "Jimmy Carter: The Religious Issue Revisited." Humanist 36 (July/August 1976): 34-35.

K12 Menendez, Albert J.   "Will Evangelicals Swing the Election?" Christianity Today 20 (June 18, 1976): 32-33.

K13 Mims, Forrest M.   "The Jimmy Carter Candidacy: Sobering Implications for Southern Baptist?" Baptist New Mexican 64 (May 29, 1976):

K14   Montgomery, Dave. "Sweeping the Baptist Vote." <u>Dallas</u>
      <u>Times-Herald</u> (May 9, 1976).

K15   Nielsen, Niels. <u>The Religion of President Carter</u>. Nashville:
      Thomas Nelson, 1977.

K16   Norton, Howard and Bob Schlosser. <u>The Miracle of Jimmy Carter</u>.
      Plainfield: Logos, 1976.

K17   Pippert, Wesley, ed. <u>The Spiritual Journey of Jimmy Carter</u>.
      New York: Macmillan, 1979.

K18   Reeves, Richard. "Is Jimmy Carter Good for the Jews?"
      <u>New York</u> 11 (May 24, 1976): 22-24.

SECTION L
THE INTERFAITH CLASH OVER CONVERSION

The bitter conflict over "range-stealing," or attempts by one religious group to convert members of another has been a repetitive source of tension in American life.

In the broadest sense it has been a Protestant vs. Catholic problem, though individual Protestant groups have fought among themselves.

This section begins with a representative sampling of conversion literature. In the "Pro-Catholic" area the most dramatic and stylistically pleasing selections are L12, L24, L29, L55, L97 and L39. On the "Anti-Catholic" side L176 is a classic of vituperative, polemical literature while L219 represents a liberal posture.

The second portion of this section includes some periodical literature probing the conversionist movements within Catholicism and Protestantism and showing how tensions increased dramatically as a result.

Pro-Catholic

L1 Adams, Elizabeth Laura. Dark Symphony. New York: Sheed and Ward, 1942.

L2 Allies, Thomas William. A Life's Decision. London: 1880.

L3 Angell, Charles and Charles La Fontaine. Prophet of Renunion. New York: Seabury, 1975.

L4 Anson, Peter Frederick. A Roving Recluse. Cork: Mercier, 1946.

L5 Armstrong, April Ousler. House with a Hundred Gates. New York: McGraw-Hill, 1965.

L6 Baker, Gladys. I Had to Know. New York: Appleton, 1951.

L7 Ballantyne, Murray. All or Nothing. New York: Sheed and and Ward, 1956.

L8 Barreau, Jean Claude. The Faith of a Pagan. New York: Paulist, 1968.

L9 Barres, Oliver. One Shepherd, One Flock. New York: Sheed and Ward, 1956.

L10 Barrett, E. Boyd. Shepherds in the Mist. Milwaukee: Bruce, 1949.

L11 Bennett, A. H. Through an Anglican Sisterhood to Rome. New York: Longmans Green, 1914.

L12   Benson, Robert Hugh. <u>Confessions of a Convert</u>. London:
      Longmans, 1913.

L13   Brown, Laurence Oliver. <u>Tadpoles and God</u>. London:
      Nicholson and Watson, 1934.

L14   Brownson, Orestes Augustus. <u>The Convert</u>. New York:
      Sadlier, 1885.

L15   Budenz, Louis. <u>This is my Story</u>. Dublin: Browne and Nolan,
      1948. New York: Whittlesey House, 1947.

L16   Budenz, Margaret. <u>Streets</u>. Huntington: Our Sunday Visitor,
      1979.

L17   Buck, Jacob Reverdy. <u>A Convert-Pastor Explains</u>. New York:
      Bruce Publishing Company, 1929.

L18   Burnett, Peter Hardeman. <u>The Path Which Led a Protestant
      Lawyer to the Catholic Church</u>. New York: Benziger, 1859.

L19   Burton, Katherine. <u>The Next Thing: Autobiography and
      Reminiscences</u>. New York: Longmans Green, 1949.

L20   Burton, Katherine. <u>In No Strange Land: Some American
      Catholic Converts</u>. New York: Longmans Green, 1942.

L21   Burton, Katherine. <u>No Shadow of Turning: The Life of James
      Kent Stone</u>. New York: Longmans Green, 1944.

L22   Burton, Katherine. <u>Sorrow Built a Bridge: The Life of
      Mother Alphonsa</u> (Rose Hawthorne Lathrop). New York:
      Longmans Green, 1937.

L23   Burton, Naomi. <u>More than Sentinels</u>. Garden City: Doubleday,
      1964.

L24   Carrel, Alexis. <u>The Voyage to Lourdes</u>. New York: Harper,
      1950.

L25   Carrouges, Michel. <u>Soldier of the Spirit: The Life of
      Charles de Foucauld</u>. New York: Putnam, 1956.

L26   Cavanaugh, Arthur. <u>My Own Backyard</u>. Garden City: Doubleday,
      1962.

L27   Chesterton, Gilbert Keith. <u>The Catholic Church and Conversion</u>.
      New York: 1927.

L28   Chesterton, Gilbert Keith. <u>The Thing</u>. New York: Sheed
      and Ward, 1957.

L29 Cory, Herbert E. The Emancipation of a Free Thinker. Milwaukee: Bruce, 1941.

L30 Crosnier, Alexis. Latter-day Converts. Philadelphia: McVey, 1912.

L31 Curtis, Georgina P. Beyond the Road to Rome. St. Louis: Herder, 1914.

L32 Curtis, Georgina P. Some Roads to Rome in America. St. Louis: Herder, 1914.

L33 Day, Dorothy. From Union Square to Rome. Silver Spring: Preservation of the Faith Press, 1938.

L34 Day, Helen Caldwell. Color Ebony. New York: Sheed and Ward, 1951.

L35 De Costa, B. V. From Canterbury to Rome. New York: Christian Press Association Publishing Compny, 1902.

L36 Delany, Shelden Peabody. Why Rome. New York: Dial Press, 1930.

L37 Dorsey, Theodore Hooper. From a Far Country. Huntington: Our Sunday Visitor, 1939.

L38 Driscoll, Annette S. Literary Convert Women. Manchester: Magnificat Press, 1928.

L39 Dulles, Avery. A Testimonial to Grace. New York: Sheed and Ward, 1946.

L40 Durkin, Joseph T. General Sherman's Son. New York: Farrar, 1959.

L41 Eberhard, Martin J. God's Ways are Wonderful. St. Paul: Randall, 1905

L42 Eustace, Cecil John. House of Bread. New York: Longmans Green, 1943.

L43 Fry, Penrose. The Church Surprising. New York, Macmillan, 1930.

L44 Gamble, Anna Dill. My Road to Rome. Baltimore: 1917

L45 Goldstein, David. Campaigners for Christ. Boston: 1936.

L46 Graef, Hilda. From Fashions to the Fathers. Westminster: Newman, 1957.

L47 Graef, Hilda. The Scholar and the Cross: The Life and Works of Edith Stein. Westminster: Newman, 1955.

L48 Grant, Dorothy Fremont. <u>What Other Answer?</u> Milwaukee:
     Bruce, 1943.

L49 Griffiths, Bede. <u>The Golden String</u>. New York: Kenedy,
     1954.

L50 Hardt, Karl, ed. <u>We Are Now Catholics</u>. Westminster:
     Newman, 1959.

L51 Hasley, Lucile. <u>Reproachfully Yours</u>. New York: Sheed
     and Ward, 1949.

L52 Hayes, Alice Jeannette. <u>A Convert's Reason Why</u>. Cambridge:
     Riverside, 1911.

L53 Hilliard, Marion Pharo. <u>The Gracious Years</u>. Paterson:
     St. Anthony Guild, 1936.

L54 Hitchcock, George S. <u>A Pilgrim of Eternity</u>. St. Louis:
     Herder, 1912.

L55 Hoffman, Ross J. <u>Restoration</u>. New York: Sheed and Ward,
     1934.

L56 Holden, Vincent F. <u>The Yankee Paul: Isaac Thomas Hecker</u>.
     Milwaukee, Bruce, 1958.

L57 Houselander, Frances Caryll. <u>A Rocking Horse Catholic</u>.
     New York: Sheed and Ward, 1955.

L58 Hulme, Kathryn Cavarly. <u>Undiscovered Country</u>. Boston:
     Little, Brown, 1966.

L59 Huntington, Joshua. <u>Gropings after Truth</u>. New York:
     Catholic Publication Society, 1858.

L60 Hyde, Douglas A. <u>I Believed</u>. New York: Putnam, 1950.

L61 Ineson, George. <u>Community Journey</u>. New York: Sheed and
     Ward, 1956.

L62 Iswolsky, Helene. <u>Light Before Dusk</u>. New York: Longmans
     Green, 1942.

L63 Ives, Levi Silliman. <u>The Trials of a Mind on its Progress
     to Catholicism</u>. Boston: Patrick Donahue, 1854.

L64 James, Bruno Scott. <u>Asking for Trouble</u>. New York: Harper,
     1963.

L65 Jeffries, Betty Jean. <u>From the Other Side</u>. Milwaukee:
     Bruce, 1955.

L66 Johnson, Vernon. *One Lord, One Faith*. London: 1929.
(new edition, London: Sheed and Ward, 1973).

L67 Kane, George Louis. *Twice Called*. Milwaukee: Bruce, 1959.

L68 Kaye-Smith, Sheila. *Three Ways Home*. New York: Harper, 1937.

L69 Kernan, William C. *My Road to Certainty*. New York: McKay,
1953.

L70 Keyes, Frances Parkinson. *Along a Little Way*. New York:
Hawthorne, 1962.

L71 Kinsman, Frederick Joseph. *Salve Mater*. New York:
Longmans Green, 1920.

L72 Knox, Ronald A. *A Spiritual Aeneid*. London and New York:
Longmans, 1918. London and New York: Sheed and Ward, 1958.

L73 Kobbe, Carolyn Therese. *My Spiritual Pilgrimage*. New York:
Devin-Adair, 1935.

L74 Kolbe, Frederick Charles. *Up the Slopes of Mount Sion; a
Progress from Puritanism to Catholicism*. New York: Benziger,
1924.

L75 Lamb, George R. *Roman Road*. New York: Sheed and Ward, 1950.

L76 Lamping, Severin, ed. *Through Hundred Gates*. Milwaukee:
Bruce, 1939.

L77 Leigh, Margaret Mary. *The Fruit in the Seed*. New York:
Sheed and Ward, 1952.

L78 Lepp, Ignace. *From Karl Marx to Jesus Christ*. New York:
Sheed and Ward, 1958.

L79 Levy, Rosalie Marie. *The Heavenly Road*. New York: 1923.

L80 Levy, Rosalie Marie. *Judaism and Catholicism*. New York:
1927.

L81 Levy, Rosalie Marie. *Thirty Years with Christ*. New York:
1943.

L82 Lockhart, William. *Conversion of Marie Alphonse Ratisbonne*.
New York: Dunigan and Brothers, 1856.

L83 Long, Valentine, ed. *They Have Seen His Star*. Paterson:
St. Anthony Guild Press, 1938.

L84 Lunn, Arnold. *And Yet So New*. New York: Sheed and Ward, 1959.

L85 Lunn, Arnold. <u>Now I See</u>. New York: Sheed and Ward, 1930.

L86 Lunn, Arnold. <u>Roman Converts</u>. New York: Scribners, 1925.

L87 Lunn, Arnold. <u>Within That City</u>. New York: Sheed and Ward, 1936.

L88 MacGillivray, George John. <u>Through the East to Rome</u>. New York: Benziger, 1932.

L89 Manning, Henry Edward (Cardinal). <u>The Religion of a Traveler</u>. San Francisco: 1897.

L90 Mannix, Edward J. <u>The American Convert Movement</u>. New York: Devin-Adair, 1923.

L91 Maritain, Raissa. <u>Adventures in Grace</u>. New York: Longmans Green, 1945.

L92 Maritain, Raissa. <u>We Have Been Friends Together</u>. New York: Longmans Green, 1942.

L93 Maynard, Theodore. <u>Orestes Brownson: Yankee, Radical, Catholic</u>. New York: Macmillan, 1943.

L94 Maynard, Theodore. <u>The World I Saw</u>. Milwaukee: Bruce, 1938.

L95 McSorley, Joseph. <u>Father Hecker and His Friends</u>. St. Louis: Herder, 1959.

L96 Melville, Annabelle M. <u>Elizabeth Bayley Seton</u>. New York: Scribners, 1951.

L97 Merton, Thomas. <u>The Seven Story Mountain</u>. New York: Harcourt, 1948.

L98 Moody, John. <u>The Long Road Home</u>. New York: Macmillan, 1936.

L99 Morrisey, Helen. <u>Ethan Allen's Daughter</u>. Gardendale, Quebec: Garden City Press, 1940.

L100 Mould, Daphne. <u>The Rock of Truth</u>. New York: Sheed and Ward, 1953.

L101 Mullen, James H. <u>Against the Goad</u>. Milwaukee: Bruce, 1961.

L102 Murdick, Olin John. <u>Journey into Truth</u>. New York: Exposition Press, 1958.

L103 Murray, Rosalind. <u>The Good Pagan's Failure</u>. New York: 1939.

L104 Newman, John Henry (Cardinal). <u>Apologia Pro Vita Sua</u>. Many editions.

L105 O'Brien, John. Giants of the Faith. New York: Doubleday, 1957.

L106 O'Brien, John A., ed. Paths to Christ. Huntington, Indiana: Our Sunday Visitor, 1945.

L107 O'Brien, John A., ed. The Road to Damascus. New York: Doubleday, 1949.

L108 O'Brien, John A., ed. Roads to Rome. New York: Macmillan, 1954.

L109 O'Brien, John A., ed. The Way to Emmaus. New York: McGraw-Hill, 1953.

L110 O'Brien, John A., ed. Where Dwellest Thou? New York: Gilbert Press, 1956.

L111 O'Brien, John A., ed. Where I Found Christ. New York: Doubleday, 1950.

L112 O'Brien, John A. The White Harvest; a Symposium on Methods of Convert Making. New York, Longmans Green, 1927.

L113 Oddo, Gilbert L., ed. These Came Home. Milwaukee: Bruce, 1954.

L114 Oesterreicher, John M., ed. Walls are Crumbling. New York: Devin-Adair, 1952.

L115 O'Hara, Constance Marie. Heaven Was Not Enough. New York: Lippincott, 1955.

L116 Orchard, William Edwin. From Faith to Faith. New York: Harper, 1933.

L117 Raupert, J. Godfrey, ed. Roads to Rome. St. Louis: Herder, 1908.

L118 Raupert, J. Godfrey. Ten Years in Anglican Orders. London: Catholic Truth Society, 1897.

L119 Raupert, J. Godfrey. From Geneva to Rome via Canterbury. New York: Benziger, 1910.

L120 Rebesher, Conrad F. Convert Making. New York: Bruch, 1937.

L121 Riach, John M. From One Convert to Another. Chicago: J. S. Paluch, 1946.

L122 Rich, Edward Charles. Seeking the City. London: Burns and Oates, 1959.

L123   Richards, Joseph Havens. <u>A Loyal Life; a Biography of
       Henry Livingston Richards</u>. St. Louis: Herder, 1913.

L124   Richards, William. <u>On the Road to Rome</u>. New York:
       Benziger, 1895.

L125   St. Aubyn, Gwendolen. <u>Towards a Pattern</u>. New York:
       Longmans Green, 1940.

L126   Sargent, Daniel. <u>Mitri: The Story of Prince Demetrius
       Augustine Gallitzin</u>. New York: Longmans Green, 1945.

L127   Scannell-O'Neill, D. J. <u>Converts to Rome in America</u>.
       Detroit: 1921.

L128   Scannell-O'Neill, D. J. <u>Distinguished Converts to Rome in
       America</u>. St. Louis: Herder, 1908.

L129   Schafer, Bruno. <u>They Heard His Voice</u>. New York: McMullen,
       1952.

L130   Scott, Martin J. <u>Christ or Chaos</u>. New York: P. J. Kenedy,
       1924.

L131   Shaw, Henry B. <u>In the Shadow of Peter</u>. Paterson: St.
       Anthony Guild, 1950.

L132   Sholl, Anna McClure. <u>The Ancient Journey</u>. New York:
       Longmans Green, 1917.

L133   Sih, Paul. <u>From Confucius to Christ</u>. New York: Sheed
       and Ward, 1952.

L134   Simon, M. Raphael. <u>The Glory of Thy People</u>. New York:
       Macmillan, 1948.

L135   Smalley, Julia C. <u>The Young Converts - Memoirs of Debbie,
       Helen and Anna Barlow</u>. New York: O'Shea, 1861.

L136   Spalding, James Field. <u>The World's Unrest and its Remedy</u>.
       New York: Longmans Green, 1898.

L137   Stancourt, Louis Joseph. <u>Her Glimmering Tapers</u>. New York:
       Macmillan, 1943.

L138   Stanton, A. J. Francis. <u>Impressions of a Pilgrim</u>. New York:
       P. J. Kenedy, 1930.

L139   Stern, Gladys B. <u>All in Good Time</u>. New York: Sheed and
       Ward, 1954.

L140   Stern, Gladys B. <u>The Way it Worked Out</u>. New York: Sheed
       and Ward, 1957.

L141   Stern, Karl. The Pillar of Fire. New York: Harcourt, Brace,
       1951.

L142   Stoddard, Charles Warren. A Troubled Heart and How It Was
       Comforted at Last. Notre Dame, Indiana: J.A. Lyons, 1885.

L143   Stoddard, John L. Rebuilding a Lost Faith. New York: Kenedy,
       1922.

L144   Stoddard, John L. Twelve Years in the Catholic Church. New
       York: Kenedy, 1930.

L145   Stone, James Kent. An Awakening and What Followed. Notre
       Dame: Ave Maria, 1919.

L146   Stone, James Kent. The Invitation Heeded: Reasons for a
       Return to Catholic Unity. New York: Christian Press, 1870.

L147   Succop, Margaret Phillips. No Going Back. Fresno: Academy
       Guild, 1964.

L148   Tarry, Ellen. The Third Door. New York: David McKay, 1955.

L149   Thomson, Paul Van Kuykendall. Why I am a Catholic. New
       York: Nelson, 1959.

L150   Treacy, James J. Conquests of Our Holy Faith. New York:
       Pustet, 1907.

L151   Vandon, Elizabeth. Late Dawn. New York: Sheed and Ward, 1958.

L152   Verkade, Willibrord. Yesterdays of an Artist-Monk. New York:
       P. J. Kenedy, 1930.

L153   Von Ruville, Albert. Back to Holy Church. New York: Longmans
       Green, 1911.

L154   Wadham, Juliana. The Case of Cornelia Connelly. New York:
       Pantheon, 1957.

L155   Ward, Maisie, ed. The English Way. New York: Sheed and Ward,
       1933.

L156   Waugh, Evelyn. Monsignor Ronald Knox. New York: Little,
       Brown, 1960.

L157   Wicklow, William Cecil. Rome is Home. Fresno: Academy
       Library Guild, 1959.

L158   Williams, Michael. The Book of the High Romance. New York:
       Macmillan, 1918.

L159   Williamson, Hugh Ross. The Walled Garden. New York:
       Macmillan, 1957.

L160   Wu, John. Beyond East and West. New York: Sheed and Ward,
       1951.

L161   Wynne, Frances. Eastward of All. Dublin: M. H. Gill, 1945.

L162   Wynne, Frances. The True Level. Dublin: M. H. Gill, 1947.

L163   Zolli, Eugenio. Before the Dawn. New York: Sheed and Ward,
       1954.

Anti-Catholic

L164   Abel, Theodore. Protestant Home Missions to Catholic Immi-
       grants. New York: Institute of Social and Religious
       Research, 1933.

L165   Aldama, Manuel. From Roman Priest to Radio Evangelist.
       Grand Rapids: Zondervan, 1946.

L166   Amand de Mendieta, Emmanuel. Rome and Canterbury. London:
       Herbert Jenkins, 1962.

L167   Arrien, Rose Fe. A Priest Renounces Celibacy (also published
       as I Married a Priest). California: Monterey Park, 1951.

L168   Bain, J. A. The New Reformation. Edinburgh: 1906.

L169   Bayssiere, Pierre. A Letter to my Children on the Subject
       of my Conversion from the Romish Church, in which I was
       Born, to the Protestant, in which I Hope to Die. London:
       1829.

L170   Blanchette, Charles Alphonse. My Reasons for Leaving the
       Roman Catholic Church. Minneapolis: 1929.

L171   Bretschneider, Karl. To Rome and Back Again. Baltimore:
       T. N. Kurtz, 1856.

L172   Calhoun, S. F. Fifteen Years in the Church of Rome.
       Lowell, Massachusetts: Vox Populi, 1886.

L173   Capes, John Morre. Reasons for Returning to the Church of
       England. London: Strahan, 1871.

L174   Carrara, John. Out of the Wilderness. Grand Rapids:
       Zondervan, 1940.

L175   Carrara, John. Why A Preacher and Not a Priest. Grand
       Rapids: Zondervan, 1946.

L176   Chiniquy, Charles. Fifty Years in the Church of Rome. New
       York: Revell, 1886.

L177   Chiniquy, Charles. <u>Forty Years in the Church of Christ</u>.
        New York: Revell, 1901.

L178   Connelly, Pierce. <u>Reasons for Abjuring Allegiance to the
        See of Rome</u>. London: 1852.

L179   Culleton, John. <u>Ten Years a Priest</u>. Louisville: 1893.

L180   Cusack, M. Francis Clare. <u>Life Inside the Church of Rome</u>.
        London: Hodder and Stoughton, 1889.

L181   Czechowski, Michael B. <u>Thrilling and Instructive Developments</u>.
        Boston: 1862.

L182   Davis, Charles. <u>A Question of Conscience</u>. New York: Harper
        and Row, 1967.

L183   Dempster, Joseph S. <u>From Romanism to Pentecost</u>. Cincinnati:
        Pentecostal Holiness Library, 1898.

L184   Donnelly, John. <u>Fifteen Years Behind the Curtains</u>. Pittsburgh:
        1896.

L185   Doyle, Sir Arthur Conan. <u>The Roman Catholic Church: A
        Rejoinder</u>. London: Psychic Press, 1930.

L186   Duval, Francis. <u>Reasons for Refusing to Continue a Member
        of the Church of Rome</u>. London: 1846.

L187   Ewin, Wilson. <u>Leading Roman Catholics to Christ</u>. Dublin:
        Christian Publications Centre, 1964.

L188   Flock, Alcyon Ruth. <u>A Brand from the Burning</u>. Mountain View,
        California: Pacific Press, 1960.

L189   Gavazzi, Alessandro. <u>Life and Lectures</u>. New York:
        DeWitt and Davenport, 1853.

L190   Halbleib, Augustus J. <u>The Autobiography of a Fallen Christ</u>.
        Richmond: Haltina, 1927.

L191   Hampel, Harry. <u>My Deliverance from the Heresies of Rome</u>.
        Dayton, Ohio: n.d.

L192   Hegger, H. T. <u>I Saw the Light</u>. Philadelphia: Presbyterian
        and Reformed, 1961.

L193   Houtin, Albert. <u>The Life of a Priest</u>. London: 1927.

L194   Hunkey, John. <u>How I became a Non-Catholic</u>. Cincinnati:
        Standard, 1911.

L195   Isaacson, Charles Stuteville, ed. <u>Roads from Rome</u>. London:
        Religious Tract Society, 1903.

L196   Kavanaugh, James. A Modern Priest Looks at his Outdated
       Church. New York: Trident, 1967.

L197   Lacueva, Francisco. From Darkness to Light. Belfast:
       Evangelical Protestant Society, 1969.

L198   Leahey, Edward. Narrative of the Conversion of the Writer
       from Romanism to the Christian Religion. Philadelphia: 1846.

L199   Lehmann, Leo H. Ex-priest and the Riddle of Religion. New
       York: Agora, Flushing, 1932.

L200   Lehmann, Leo H. The Soul of a Priest. Sea Cliff, New York:
       Christ's Mission, 1933.

L201   Longo, Gabriel. Spoiled Priest. New Hyde Park, New York:
       University Books, 1966. (Paperback edition - Bantam,
       New York: 1967).

L202   McCabe, Joseph. Twelve Years in a Monastery. London:
       C. A. Watts, 1930.

L203   McCabe, Joseph. Why I Left the Church. New York: Free-
       thought Press Association, 1897.

L204   McGerald, Samuel. Reasons Why I Cannot Return to the Church
       of Rome. Buffalo: True Faith Company, 1915.

L205   McLoughlin, Emmett. Famous Ex-Priests. New York: Lyle
       Stuart, 1968.

L206   McLoughlin, Emmett. People's Padre. Boston: Beacon, 1954.

L207   Malinverni, Aristide. My Conversion and Reasons That Led
       to It. Los Angeles: Everlasting Gospel, 1922.

L208   Mayerhoffer, Vincent Philip. Twelve Years a Roman Catholic
       Priest. Toronto: Rowsell and Ellis, 1861.

L209   O'Connor, James A. Letters to Cardinal McCloskey. New York:
       "Converted Catholic" Publishing Office, 1884.

L210   O'Gorman, W. E. R. A Priest Speaks his Mind. Glendale,
       California: 1954.

L211   Padrosa, Luis. Why I Became a Protestant. Moody, Chicago: 1953.

L212   Pearson, B. H. The Monk Who Lived Again. Los Angeles: Cowman
       1940.

L213   Pepin, Francois. A Narrative of the Life and Experiences of
       Francois Pepin who was for more than Forty Years a Member of
       the Papl Church, Embracing an Account of his Conversion,
       Trials and Persecutions in Turning to the True Religion
       of the Bible. Detroit: 1854.

L214 Poynter, J. M. Inside the Roman Church by One Who Was There.
      London, Epworth: 1930.

L215 Santorio, Enrico C. Social and Religious Life of Italians
      in America. Boston: 1918.

L216 Seguin, P. A. Out of Hell and Purgatory. Stevens Point,
      Wisconsin: 1912.

L217 Smith, Samuel B. Renunciation of Popery. Philadelphia: 1833.

L218 Sullivan, William Laurence. Letters to His Holiness Pope
      Pius X. Chicago: Open Court, 1910.

L219 Sullivan, William Laurence. Under Orders. New York:
      Richard R. Smith, 1945.

L220 Vila, Manuel Perez. I Found the Ancient Way. Chicago:
      Moody, 1958.

L221 Vinet, Lucien. I Was a Priest. Toronto and Winnipeg:
      Canadian Protestant League, 1949.

L222 Von Hoensbroech, Count Paul. Fourteen Years a Jesuit.
      New York: 1911.

L223 Von Kubinyi, Victor. Behind the Curtain. Chicago: Seemore,
      1913.

L224 Von Kubinyi, Victor. Through Fog to Light. South Bend:
      Seemore, 1914.

L225 Von Zedtqitz, Baroness. The Double Doctrine of the Church
      of Rome. New York: Revell, 1906.

L226 Walsh, Lilian A. My Hand in His. Worthing, England: Henry
      E. Walter, Ltd., 1957.

L227 Walsh, Lilian A. Wonderful Name. Worthing, England: Henry
      E. Walter, Ltd., 1967.

L228 Witcutt, W. P. Return to Reality. London: S.P.C.K., 1954.

The Conversionist Movements

L229   Barrois, G. A.   "My Spiritual Journey from Catholicism to
       Protestantism."   Christian Century 66 (June 1, 1949):
       676-678.

L230   Bernarding, Peter J.   "Catholic Losses in the United States
       During 1930."   American Ecclesiastical Review 86 (1932):
       135-148.

L231   Brewer, Bartholomew.   Pilgrimage From Rome.   Greenville,
       South Carolina: Bob Jones University Press, 1983.

L232   Browne, Henry J.   "The 'Italian Problem' in the Catholic
       Church of the United States, 1880-1900."   United States
       Catholic Historical Society Records and Studies 35 (1946):
       46-72.

L233   Burke, T. J. M.   "Did Four Million Catholics Become Protestants?"
       America 91 (April 10, 1954): 37-39.

L234   Canavan, Mary Elizabeth.   "The Appeal of Catholic Mysticism
       to New England Protestants of the Early Nineteenth Century
       and the Conversions It Inspired."   M.A. thesis.   Boston
       College, 1932.

L235   Canevin, J. F. Regis.   "Loss and Gain in the Catholic Church
       in the United States, 1800-1916."   Catholic Historical
       Review 2 (1917): 377-385.

L236   "Catholic Leakage: Chicago Survey Findings."   America 112
       (June 12, 1965): 846.

L237   "Catholic Losses in America."   United States Catholic Historical
       Magazine 4 (1891-1892): 70-90.

L238   Caylor, John.   In Evangeline's Country.   Atlanta: Southern
       Baptist Convention Home Mission Board, 1950.

L239   Clarke, Richard.   "Our Converts."   American Catholic Quarterly
       Review XVIII (July 1893): 539-561; XIX (January 1894): 112-138.

L240   "Conversion Poll Ends in a Dead Heat."   Christian Century 72
       (April 6, 1955): 411.

L241   Curtis, Georgina P.   "Early Conversions to the Catholic Church
       in America."   Catholic Historical Review 1 (1916): 271-281.

L242   Desmond, Humphrey J.   "Fallen-Away Catholics in America."
       Catholic World 117 (August 1923): 577-590.

L243   Gibson, Sister Laurita.   Some Anglo-American Converts to
       Catholicism Prior to 1829.   Washington: Catholic University,
       1943.

L244 Griffin, Clifford S. "Converting the Catholics: American
      Benevolent Societies and the Ante-Bellum Crusade against
      the Church." Catholic Historical Review 47 (1961): 325-341.

L245 High, S. "Catholic Converts." Current History 52 (September
      1940): 29-31.

L246 Hudson, Withrop S. "Roads That Lead to Rome." Christian
      Century 66 (December 7, 1949): 1452-1453.

L247 Jenkins, Mary Lou and Hannah E. Reynolds. God's Dividends
      in Louisiana. Alexandria: Baptist Women's Missionary Union,
      1950.

L248 Luce, Clare Booth. "The Catholic Mind and the Protestant
      Heart." Catholic World 174 (January 1952): 246-253.

L249 Lucey, William L. "Some Catholic Converts." Records of the
      American Catholic Historical Society of Philadephia 67
      (1956): 67-87.

L250 O'Brien, John A. "Convert Decline." America 109 (October 5,
      1963): 382.

L251 O'Brien, John A. "Operation Doorbell in Louisiana." America
      94 (February 4, 1956): 501-503.

L252 Oursler, Fulton. "Return to Reality." Christian Century
      66 (May 18, 1949): 623-625.

L253 Routh, Porter. "Are Catholics Winning the South?" The
      Quarterly Review VIII (January-March 1948): 21-25.

L254 Shea, John Gilmary. "Converts--Their Influence and Work
      in This Country." American Catholic Quarterly Review
      8 (1883): 525.

L255 Wynn, J. C. "Roads to Rome." Christian Century 68 (February
      7, 1951): 171-172.

SECTION M
THE CONTINUING CONTROVERSY OVER GOVERNMENT AID
TO RELIGIOUS SCHOOLS

The controversy over government aid to parochial schools goes back to the 1840s in New York State, when Catholics and Protestants clashed politically over this volatile issue. The result was the Catholic Church's commitment to an independent school system deprived of any public subsidy. Protestants supported the emerging public school system, though in many localities they attempted to make the public schools Protestant in tone.

Liberal and progressive forces opposed both public aid to sectarian schools and Protestant bias in the publicly-provided schools. At the same time half or more of the nation's Catholics sent their children to public schools, and a small but growing minority of Protestant evangelicals preferred parochial education.

Support for "parochiaid" can be seen in M1, M2, M9-12, M24, M39, M64, M70, M80, M85, M119, M14, M15, M46, M57.

The case against parochiaid is mounted in M19, M92, M23, M32, M77, M21, M72, M74, M128, M93, and M76.

Some essential historical background can be obtained in M49, M59, M66, M31, M47, M52, M73, M105.

The nature of parochial education is explored in M103, M107, M118, M137, M6, M13, M16, M17, M18, M25, M40, M48, M53, M54, M65, M68, M81-87, M99, M97, M100, M109, M112, M115 and M131.

The famous Oregon school crisis of the 1920s, when all parochial and private schools were nearly abolished, is examined by M60, M61 and M125.

An excellent case study of parochial school busing in Connecticut is found in M104.

M1 Ball, William B. "Family Freedom in Education." The Human Life Review 6 (Summer 1980): 60-69.

M2 Ball, William B. "Religious Liberty in Education." Journal of Ecumenical Studies 14 (Fall 1977): 662-676.

M3 Bartell, Ernest. Costs and Benefits of Catholic Elementary and Secondary Schools. Notre Dame: University of Notre Dame, 1969.

M4 Bayly, Joseph. "Private Schools, Public Tax." Eternity 29 (May 1978): 71-72.

M5 Beach, Fred Francis and Robert F. Will. The State and Nonpublic Schools. Washington, D.C.: U.S. Department of Health, Education, and Welfare, 1958.

M6   Beck, Walter H. Lutheran Elementary Schools in the U.S.
     St. Louis: Concordia, 1939.

M7   Benjamin, Marge. Three Out of Ten: The Nonpublic Schools
     of New York City. New York: New York Department of City
     Planning, 1972.

M8   Bishop, Claire Huchet. How Catholics Look at Jews. New
     York: Paulist, 1974.

M9   Blum, Virgil C. Catholic Education: Survival or Demise?
     Chicago: Argus, 1969.

M10 Blum, Virgil C. Freedom in Education. New York: Doubleday,
     1965.

M11 Blum, Virgil C. Freedom of Choice. New York: Macmillan,
     1958.

M12 Blum, Virgil C. "Tax Refunds for Tuition." America 144
     (April 11, 1981): 294-297.

M13 Brekke, Milo. How Different Are People Who Attended
     Lutheran Schools? St. Louis: Concordia, 1974.

M14 Brickman, William W. and Stanley Lehrer, eds. Religion,
     Government and Education. New York: Society for the Advance-
     ment of Education, 1961.

M15 Bridges, L. "High Price of Fanaticism." National Review
     23 (November 19, 1971): 1297-1298.

M16 Brown, William E. and Andrew M. Greeley. Can Catholic
     Schools Survive? New York: Sheed and Ward, 1970.

M17 Buetow, Harold A. Of Singular Benefit: The Story of
     Catholic Education in the United States. New York:
     Macmillan, 1970.

M18 Burns, James A. and Bernard J. Kohlbrenner. A History of
     Catholic Education in the United States. New York:
     Benziger, 1937. (Reprint by New York: Arno Press, 1969).

M19 Butts, R. Freeman. "Education Vouchers: The Private
     Pursuit of the Public Purse." Phi Delta Kappan 61
     (September 1979): 7-9.

M20 Callahan, Daniel J., ed. Federal Aid and Catholic Schools.
     Baltimore: Helicon, 1964.

M21 "Catholics Demand Patronage." Christian Century 78 (March 22,
     1961): 381-382.

M22 Chopper, Jesse H. "The Establishment Clause and Aid to
     Parochial Schools." California Law Review 56 (1968):
     260-341.

M23 Cogdell, Gaston. What Price Parochiaid? Washington, D.C.:
     Americans United, 1968.

M24 Coons, John E. "Of Family Choice and Public Education."
     Phi Delta Kappan 61 (September 1979): 10-13.

M25 Crowley, Jeremiah. The Parochial School - A Curse to the
     Church, a Menace to the Nation. Chicago: 1905.

M26 Cupps, Terry C. "Schools: Permissibility of Direct
     Governmental Aid to Sectarian Schools." Washburn Law
     Journal 20 (Fall 1980): 178-185.

M27 Dana, Ellis H. "Mounting Church-State Issues." Education
     69 (October 1948): 124-130.

M28 Deferrari, Roy J. Complete System of Catholic Education
     is Necessary. Boston: Daughters of St. Paul, 1964.

M29 Deferrari, Roy J., ed. Vital Problems of Catholic Education
     in the United States. Washington, D.C.: Catholic University
     of America, 1939.

M30 De Hovre, Franz. Catholicism in Education. New York:
     Benziger, 1934.

M31 Diffley, Jerome E. Catholic Reaction to American Public
     Education. Notre Dame: University of Notre Dame, 1959.

M32 Doerr, Edd. The Conspiracy That Failed. Washington, D.C.:
     Americans United, 1968.

M33 Dushkin, Alexander M. Jewish Education in New York City.
     New York: Bureau of Jewish Education, 1918.

M34 Duval, Benjamin S. "Constitutionality of State Aid to
     Nonpublic Elementary and Secondary Schools." University
     of Illinois Law Forum, 1970.

M35 Duvall, Sylvanus Milne. The Methodist Episcopal Church
     and Education Up To 1869. New York: Columbia University,
     1928.

M36 Erickson, Donald A., ed. Public Controls for Nonpublic
     Schools. Chicago: University of Chicago, 1969.

M37 Evenson, J. Eric. "State Regulation of Private Religious
     Schools in North Carolina - a Model Approach." Wake
     Forest Law Review 16 (June 1980): 405-437.

M38   Farrell, Allan P. "The School Controversy (1891-1893)."
      Catholic Educational Review 43 (1945): 203-207.

M39   Ferrara, Peter J. Religion and the Constitution: A
      Reinterpretation. Washington: Free Congress Research
      and Education Foundation. 1983.

M40   Fichter, Joseph H. Parochial School: A Sociological Study.
      Notre Dame: University of Notre Dame, 1958.

M41   The Fleischmann Report on the Quality, Cost, and Financing
      of Elementary and Secondary Education in New York State.
      New York: Viking, 1973.

M42   Flowers, Ronald and Robert T. Miller. Toward Benevolent
      Neutrality. Waco: Baylor University Press, 1982.

M43   Frasca, W. R. "Confusion in the Supreme Court." Thought
      28 (Winter 1953-54): 547-570.

M44   Frey, D. E. "Parochiaid." Christian Century 90 (March 28,
      1973): 366-368.

M45   Friedlander, Anna Fay. The Shared Time Strategy: Prospects
      and Trends in the Growing Partnership Between Public and
      Church Schools. St. Louis: Concordia, 1966.

M46   Friedman, Milton and P. Binzen. "Politics and Parochiaid."
      New Republic 164 (January 23, 1971): 12-15.

M47   Gabel, Richard J. Public Funds for Church and Private Schools.
      Washington, D.C.: Catholic University of America, 1937.

M48   Gabert, Glen. In Hoc Signo?: A Brief History of Catholic
      Parochial Education in America. Port Washington, New York:
      Kennikat, 1973.

M49   Gaffney, Edward McGlynn. "Political Divisiveness Along
      Religious Lines: The Entanglement of the Court in Sloppy
      History." St. Louis University Law Journal 24 (September
      1980): 205-236.

M50   Giacoma, James M. "Pearl v. Regan: New Possibilities for
      State Aid to Private Schools." St. Louis University Law
      Journal 24 (September 1980): 401-424.

M51   Gianella, Donald A. "Lemon and Tilton: The Bitter and the
      Sweet of Church-State Entanglement." The Supreme Court
      Review (1971): 147-200.

M52   Goebel, Edmund J. A Study of Catholic Secondary Education
      During the Colonial Period up to the First Plenary Council
      of Baltimore. New York: Benziger, 1937.

M53 Greeley, Andrew M. Catholic Schools in a Declining Church. New York: Sheed and Ward, 1976.

M54 Greeley, Andrew M. and Peter H. Rossi. The Education of Catholic Americans. Chicago: Aldine, 1966.

M55 Groom, P. "Suffer the Little Non-Catholic Children." Catholic World 169 (June 1949): 198-202.

M56 Healey, Robert M. The French Achievement: Private School Aid, a Lesson for America. New York: Paulist, 1974.

M57 Herberg, Will. "Justice for Religious Schools." America 98 (November 16, 1957): 190-193.

M58 Higgins, E. A. "The American State and the Private School." Catholic World 53 (July 1891): 521-527.

M59 Hitchcock, James. "The Supreme Court and Religion: Historical Overview and Future Prognosis." St. Louis University Law Journal 24 (September 1980): 183-204.

M60 Holsinger, M. Paul. "The Oregon School Controversy, 1922-1925." Pacific Historical Review XXXVII (August 1968): 327-341.

M61 "Intolerance in Oregon." Survey XLIX (October 15, 1922): 76-77.

M62 Jellison, Helen M., ed. State and Federal Laws Relating to Nonpublic Schools. Washington, D.C.: U.S. Department of Health Education and Welfare, 1975.

M63 Kelley, Dean M. "Protestants and Parochial Schools." Commonweal 79 (January 31, 1964): 520-524.

M64 Kelly, George A., ed. Government Aid to Nonpublic Schools: Yes or No? New York: St. John's University Press, 1972.

M65 Kienel, Paul A. The Christian School: Why it is Right for Your Child. Wheaton: Victor Books, 1974.

M66 Kizer, George. "An Analysis of the Drive for Public Funds for Parochial Schools, 1945-1963." Ph.D. dissertation. University of Oklahoma, 1964.

M67 Knebel, Fletcher. "The Bishops vs. Kennedy." Look 23 (May 9, 1961): 24-26.

M68 Koob, C. Albert and Russell Shaw. S.O.S. for Catholic Schools. New York: Holt, Rinehart and Winston, 1970.

M69 Koob, C. Albert, ed. What is Happening to Catholic Education? Washington, D.C.: National Catholic Educational Association, 1966.

M70   Krasicky, Eugene. "Ride in the Back of the Bus." Catholic
      Mind 74 (April 1976): 34-43.

M71   Kraushaar, Otto F. American Nonpublic Schools. Baltimore:
      John Hopkins, 1972.

M72   Lader, Lawrence. "Hidden Threat to Education: Public Funds
      to Support Parochial Schools." Parents Magazine 43
      (September 1968): 58-61.

M73   Lannie, Vincent P. Public Money and Parochial Education:
      Bishop Hughes, Governor Seward, and the New York School
      Controversy. Cleveland: Case Western Reserve University,
      1968.

M74   LaNoue, George R. "Church, State and the Courts." Nation
      209 (December 15, 1969): 656-659.

M75   LaNoue, George R., ed. Educational Vouchers: Concepts and
      Controversies. New York: Teacher's College Press of
      Columbia University, 1972.

M76   LaNoue, George R. "Public Funds for Public Schools Only."
      Christian Century 79 (May 23, 1962): 648-649.

M77   Larson, Martin A. When Parochial Schools Close. Washington,
      D.C.: Robert B. Luce, Inc., 1972.

M78   Loughlin, James F. "The School Controversy in the United
      States." American Ecclesiastical Review 6 (1892): 119-122.

M79   McCarthy, Martha M. "Church and State: Separation or
      Accommodation?" Harvard Educational Review 51 (August
      1981): 373-394.

M80   McCarthy, Rockne M., et.al. Disestablishment a Second Time:
      Genuine Pluralism for American Schools. Grand Rapids:
      Eerdmans, 1982.

M81   McCluskey, Neil G. Catholic Education Faces its Future.
      New York: Doubleday, 1969.

M82   McCluskey, Neil G. Catholic Education in America: A
      Documentary History. Richmond: William Byrd Press, 1964.

M83   McCluskey, Neil G. Catholic Viewpoint on Education.
      Milwaukee: Bruce, 1934.

M84   McCluskey, Neil G. "How Much State Support?" America
      101 (September 19, 1959): 722-724

M85   McGarry, Daniel D. and Leo Ward. Educational Freedom and the
      Case for Government Aid to Students in Independent Schools.
      Milwaukee: Bruce, 1966.

M86   McGucken, William. The Jesuits and Education. Milwaukee:
      Bruce, 1932.

M87   McGucken, William. The Catholic Way in Education. Milwaukee:
      Bruce, 1934.

M88   McLaughlin, Raymond, Sr. A History of State Legislation
      Affecting Private Elementary and Secondary Schools in the
      United States, 1870-1945. Washington, D.C.: Catholic
      University of America, 1946.

M89   McLoughlin, Emmet. American Culture and Catholic Schools.
      New York: Lyle Stuart, 1960.

M90   McSorley, Joseph. "State Aid to Parish Schools." America
      101 (September 19, 1959): 722-724.

M91   Merk, Lois B. "Boston's Historic Public School Crisis."
      New England Quarterly 31 (1958): 172-199.

M92   Morris, Barbara M. Tuition Tax Credits: A Responsible
      Appraisal. Upland, California: Barbara Morris Report, 1983.

M93   Morrison, Charles Clayton. "Church, State and Constitution."
      Christian Century 65 (September 1, 1948): 865-868.

M94   Mullaney, T. R. "Tax Credits and Parochial Schools." Commonweal
      98 (April 27, 1973): 185-188.

M95   Mullary, J. F. Catholic Education and American Institutions.
      New York: 1898.

M96   Nault, Richard L. "Institutional Jeopardy and Government
      Funding of Catholic Schools." Momentum 12 (February 1981):
      39-41.

M97   Neuwien, Reginald A., ed. Catholic Schools in Action.
      Notre Dame and London: University of Notre Dame, 1966.

M98   O'Brien, Kenneth B., Jr. "Education, Americanization and the
      Supreme Court." American Quarterly XIII (1961): 161-171.

M99   O'Connell, Laurence John. Are Catholic Schools Progressive?
      St. Louis: B. Herder, 1946.

M100 Office for Education Research, University of Notre Dame.
      Economic Problems of Nonpublic Schools. Indiana: Notre
      Dame, 1971.

M101 Pawlikowski, John T. Catechetics and Prejudice. New York:
      Paulist Press, 1973.

M102 Phelan, Jeremiah. Which are the More Godless, the Public
      or Parochial Schools? Rochester: 1917.

M103   Plude, Frances F. What's Happening to Catholic Schools?
       New York: Sadlier, 1974.

M104   Powell, Theodore. The School Bus Law. Middletown, Connecticut:
       Wesleyan University, 1960.

M105   Pratt, John Webb. Religion, Politics and Diversity: The
       Church-State Theme in New York History. Ithaca: Cornell
       University Press, 1967.

M106   Raabe, William. "Parochial Schools and the IRS: The Scope
       of Administrative Control." Taxes 58 (July 1980): 494- 499.

M107   Rossi, Peter H. and Alice S. Rossi. "Some Effects of
       Parochial School Education in America." Daedalus 90
       (Spring 1961): 300-328.

M108   Ryan, Mary Perkins. Are Parochial Schools the Answer?
       New York: Holt, Rinehart and Winston, 1964.

M109   Ryan, Mary Perkins. We're All in This Together: Issues
       and Options in the Education of Catholics. New York:
       Holt, Rinehart and Winston, 1972.

M110   Savage, David G. "Expect a Battle over Tuition Tax Credits."
       Phi Delta Kappan 63 (February 1981): 411-412.

M111   Shaw, Russell B. "Arguments, Attitudes, and Aid."
       Momentum 6 (December 1975): 34-37.

M112   Shaw, Russell B., ed. Trends and Issues in Catholic Education.
       New York: Citation, 1969.

M113   Sheerin, John B. "Conant and Catholic Schools." Catholic
       World 175 (June 1952): 161-165.

M114   Sherrill, Lewis Joseph. Presbyterian Parochial Schools.
       New Haven: Yale University Press, 1932.

M115   Shuster, George N. Catholic Education in a Changing World.
       New York: Holt, Rinehart and Winston, 1968.

M116   Smith, E. A. "Further Proposal for Federal Aid to Catholic
       Schools." Catholic World 201 (June 1965): 162-169.

M117   Stokes, R. L. "Senator Taft on Catholic Schools." Catholic
       World 175 (July 1952): 246-250.

M118   Stravinskas, Peter M. J. Catholic Education: A New Dawn?
       Canfield, Ohio: Alba Books, 1977.

M119   Stravinskas, Peter M. J. Constitutional Rights and Religious
       Prejudice: Catholic Education as the Battleground. Milwaukee:
       Catholic League, 1983.

M120   Sullivan, Daniel J. Public Aid to Nonpublic Schools.
       Lexington, Massachusetts: D. C. Heath, 1974.

M121   Swomley, John M. "Are Parochial Schools Imperiled?" Christian
       Century 88 (January 13, 1971): 40-43.

M122   Tavel, David. Church-State Issues in Education. Bloomington:
       Phi Delta Kappa, 1979.

M123   Taylor, Judith K. "Educational Vouchers: Addressing the
       Establishing Clause." Pacific Law Journal 11 (July 1980):
       1061-1083.

M124   Thiessen, Elma J. and Roy Wilson. "Curriculum in the Church-
       State Controversy " Inform 3 (January 1981): 1-8.

M125   Tyack, D. B. "Perils of Pluralism: The Background of the
       Pierce Case." American Historical Review 75 (October 1968):
       74-98.

M126   U.S. Office of Education. Dual Enrollment in Public and
       Non-Public Schools. Washington, D.C.: U.S. Government Printing
       Office, 1965.

M127   Vilas, W. F. "The Bennent Law in Wisconsin." Forum 12
       October 1891): 196-207.

M128   "The Voucher Plan: Blueprint for Disaster." Church & State
       31 (February 1978): 7-11.

M129   Walinsky, Adam. "Aid to Parochial Schools." New Republic
       167 (October 7, 1972): 18-21.

M130   Walsh, J. E. "Parochial School: Partner or Pariah?"
       School and Society 71 (April 29, 1950): 257-262.

M131   Ward, Leo R. New Life in Catholic Schools. New York:
       Herder and Herder, 1958.

M132   Weigel, Gustave. "Religious Schools and Civic Harmony."
       Catholic World 196 (March 1963): 351-356.

M133   West, E. G. Nonpublic School Aid. Toronto: Lexington Books,
       1977.

M134   Whelan, Charles M. "The School Aid Decision." America
       131 (July 7, 1973): 6-8.

M135   Whelan, Charles M. "School Question: State Two." America
       104 (April 11, 1961): 17-19.

M136   Whelan, Charles M. "Textbooks and the Taxpayer." America
       119 (July 6, 1968): 8-11.

M137 Wilson, Ellen. Catholic Education: A Backward Look at
      the Future. New York: National Committee of Catholic
      Laymen, 1979.

SECTION N
RELIGIOUS CLASHES IN PUBLIC SCHOOLS,
INCLUDING THE BIBLE READING AND PRAYER CONTROVERSIES

No issue has been more explosive than religion in the public
school. It has literally provoked blood-in-the streets (see C34)
and bitterness which tore another large city apart (N63).

Certain selections are essential: N12, N14, N15, N22, N24,
N36, N53, N94, N100, N106, N120, and N122.

Polemical words from conservative Protestants are represented
by N8, N39, N44, N47, N51, N92, N99, N102, and N125.

How the public schools moved from a Protestant to a religiously
neutral posture is examined by N20 and N26.

Religious bias in textbooks is probed by N48, N87, N124.

Three fine bibliographies which include much additional
material are N42, N79, N108.

The dilemma of Christians in the public schools can be seen
in N25, N30, and N116.

N1 Adams, Marjorie E., ed. God in the Classroom. South
    Pasadena: National Educators Fellowship, 1970.

N2 American Association of School Administrators. Religion in
    the Public Schools. New York: Harper, 1964.

N3 American Council on Education. The Function of the Public
    Schools in Dealing with Religion. Washington, D.C.: 1953.

N4 American Council on Education. The Relation of Religion
    to Public Education. Washington, D.C.: 1947.

N5 American Council on Education. Religion and Public Education.
    Washington, D.C.: 1944.

N6 Ball, William B. "Legal Religion in the Schools." Catholic
    World 197 (September 1963): 366-371.

N7 Baltazar, E. R. "T M and the Religion-in-School Issue."
    Christian Century 93 (August 18, 1976): 708-709.

N8 Bedsole, Adolph. The Supreme Court Decision on Bible
    Reading and Prayer: America's Black Letter Day. Grand
    Rapids: Baker, 1964.

N9 Beggs, David W., ed. America's Schools and Churches; Partners
    in Conflict. Bloomington: Indiana University, 1966.

N10   Beman, Lamar Taney. Religious Teaching in the Public Schools.
      New York: H. W. Wilson, 1927.

N11   The Bible in the Public Schools. Cincinnati: Robert Clarke
      and Company, 1870. (Reprint by New York: Da Capo Press, 1967).

N12   Blanshard, Paul. Religion and the Schools. Boston: Beacon,
      1963.

N13   Bloom H. "California's Church School War." Nation 174
      (May 31, 1952): 521-522.

N14   Boles, Donald E. The Bible, Religion and the Public Schools.
      Ames: Iowa State University, 1965.

N15   Boles, Donald E. The Two Swords. Ames: Iowa State University,
      1967.

N16   Bower, William C. Moral and Spiritual Values in Education.
      Lexington: University of Kentucky, 1952.

N17   Boyer, W. W. "Baccalaureate in Brodhead: A Study of Inter-
      faith Tension." School and Society 88 (April 9, 1960):
      183-186.

N18   Braiterman, Marvin. Religion and the Public Schools. New
      York: American Jewish Committee, 1958.

N19   Brant, Irving. "Madison and the Prayer Case." New Republic
      147 (July 30, 1962): 18-20.

N20   Brown, Samuel Windsor. The Secularization of American
      Education. New York: Columbia University Press, 1912.
      (Reprint by New York: AMS Press, 1972).

N21   Brubacher, John S., ed. The Public Schools and Spiritual
      Values. New York: Harper, 1944.

N22   Butts, R. Freeman. The American Tradition in Religion and
      Education. Boston: Beacon, 1950.

N23   Buddy, C. F. "Bring the Ten Commandments Back into the Schools."
      America 93 (September 24, 1955): 613-615.

N24   Byrnes, Lawrence. Religion and Public Education. New York:
      Harper and Row, 1975.

N25   "Christmas in the Schools." NEA Journal 56 (December 1967):
      54-57.

N26   Confrey, Burton. Secularism in American Education - Its
      History. Washington, D.C.: Catholic University of America,
      1931.

N27 Coogan, J. E. "That Wall of Separation and the Public
     Schools." Catholic World 172 (January 1951): 252-255.

N28 Coxe, Claire. The Fourth R: What Can be Taught about
     Religion in the Public Schools. New York: Hawthorn, 1969.

N29 Cubberley, Ellwood P. "Battle to Eliminate Sectarianism
     in Public Schools." NEA Journal 41 (April 1952): 228-230.

N30 Culligan, G. "Bah, Humbug: Christmas Poses Dilemma for
     the Schools." American Education 3 (December 1966): 14-17.

N31 Culver, Raymond B. Horace Mann and Religion in the Massachusetts
     Public Schools. New Haven: Yale University Press, 1929.

N32 Davis, Mary Dabney. Week-Day Religious Instruction.
     Washington, D.C.: U.S. Government Printing Office, 1933.

N33 Davis, Mary Dabney. Week-Day Classes in Religious Education.
     Washington, D.C.: U.S. Government Printing Office, 1941.

N34 Department of Elementary School Principals. Spiritual Values
     in the Elementary School. Washington, D.C.: National
     Education Association, 1947.

N35 Dieffenbach, Albert C. Religious Liberty: The Great
     American Illusion. New York: 1927.

N36 Dierenfield, Richard B. Religion in American Public Schools.
     Washington, D.C.: Public Affairs Press, 1962.

N37 Diffley, Jerome E. "Catholic Reaction to American Public
     Education, 1792-1852." Ph.D. dissertation. University
     of Notre Dame, 1959.

N38 Dolbeare, Kenneth and Phillip Hammond. The School Prayer
     Decisions. Chicago: University of Chicago, 1971.

N39 Dorchester, Daniel. Romanism Versus the Public School System.
     New York: Phillips and Hunt, 1888.

N40 Douglas, William O. The Bible and the Schools. Boston:
     Little, Brown and Company, 1966.

N41 Drinan, Robert F. "Prayer in the Public School." America
     102 (October 17, 1959): 70-71.

N42 Drouin, Edmond G. The School Question: A Bibliography on
     Church-State Relationships in American Education, 1940-1960.
     Washington, D.C.: Catholic University of America, 1963.

N43 Duker, Sam. The Public Schools and Religion: The Legal
     Context. New York: Harper, 1966.

N44   Dunn, James B. The Pope's Last Veto in American Politics.
      Boston: Committee of One Hundred, 1890.

N45   Dunn, William K. What Happened to Religious Education?
      Baltimore: Johns Hopkins University Press, 1958.

N46   Educational Policies Commission. Moral and Spiritual Values
      in the Public Schools. Washington, D.C.: National Education
      Association, 1951.

N47   Ellis, Samuel Moore. The Bible Indispensable in Education.
      Pittsburgh: National Reform Association, 1926.

N48   Elson, Ruth Miller. Guardians of Tradition: American School-
      books of the Nineteenth Century. Lincoln: University of
      Nebraska Press, 1964.

N49   Engel, David E., ed. Religion in Public Education. Paramus,
      New Jersey: Paulist, 1974.

N50   Engel, H. M. "School Prayer Issue, a Perverse Paradox."
      Catholic World 211 (June 1970): 125-127.

N51   Fleming, W. S. God in Our Public Schools. Pittsburgh:
      National Reform Association, 1942.

N52   Forman, B. J. "Are Jewish Children Left Out?" Scholastic
      Arts 57 (December 1957): 25-28.

N53   Freund, Paul A. and Robert Ulich. Religion and the Public
      Schools. Cambridge: Harvard University Press, 1965.

N54   Frommer, Arthur, ed. The Bible and the Public Schools.
      New York: Frommer, 1963.

N55   Gobbell, L. L. Church and State Relationships in Education
      in North Carolina Since 1776. Durham: Duke University, 1938.

N56   Gordis, Robert T., et.al. Religion and the Schools. Santa
      Barbara: Fund for the Republic, 1959.

N57   Gove, Floyd S. Religious Education on Public School Time.
      Cambridge: Harvard University, 1926.

N58   Hall, Arthur Jackson. Religious Education in the Public
      Schools of the State and City of New York. Chicago:
      University of Chicago, 1914.

N59   Hall, Christopher. The Christian Teacher and the Law.
      Oak Park, Illinois: Christian Legal Society, 1975.

N60   Hauser, Conrad A. Teaching Religion in the Public School.
      New York: Round Table Press, 1942.

N61 Hay, C. L. The Blind Spot in American Public Education.
     New York: Macmillan, 1950.

N62 Healey, Robert M. Jefferson on Religion in Public Education.
     New Haven: Yale University Press, 1962.

N63 Helfman, Harold M. "The Cincinnati Bible War, 1869-1870."
     Ohio State Archaeological and Historical Quarterly 60
     (October 1951): 369-386.

N64 Helmreich, Ernst C. Religion and the Main Schools: An
     Historical Approach. Brunswick, Maine: Bureau for Research
     in Municipal Government, 1960.

N65 Henry, Virgil. The Place of Religion in Public Schools.
     New York: Harper, 1950.

N66 Holtz, Adrian Augustus. A Study of the Moral and Religious
     Elements in American Secondary Education up to 1800.
     Menasha, Wisconsin: 1917.

N67 Hood, William R. The Bible in the Public Schools, Legal Status
     and Current Practice. Washington, D.C.: U.S. Government
     Printing Office, 1923.

N68 Hubner, Sister Mary. Professional Attitudes Toward Religion
     in the Public Schools of the U.S. since 1900. Washington,
     D.C.: Catholic University of America, 1944.

N69 Hunt, R. L. "Teaching about Religion in the Public School."
     Today's Education 58 (December 1969): 24-26.

N70 Hurley, Mark J. Church-State Relationships in Education in
     California. Washington, D.C.: Catholic University of
     America, 1948.

N71 Jackson, Jerome Case and Constantine Malmberg. Religious
     Education and the State. Garden City: Doubleday, Doran, 1928.

N72 Johnson, Alvin W. The Legal Status of Church-State Relation-
     ships in the U.S., with Special Reference to the Public
     Schools. Minneapolis: University of Minnesota Press, 1934.

N73 Johnson, F. Ernest, ed. American Education and Religion.
     New York: Harper, 1952.

N74 Jones, Alonzo T. The Place of the Bible in Education.
     Oakland: Pacific Press, 1903.

N75 Kerlinger, F. N. "Religious Displays and Public Education."
     School and Society 90 (April 21, 1962): 196-198.

N76   Lardner, L. A. "How Far Does the Constitution Separate Church
      and State?" American Political Science Review 45 (March
      1951): 110-132.

N77   Laubach, John H. School Prayers: Congress, the Courts, and
      the Public. Washington, D.C.: Public Affairs Press, 1969.

N78   Levy, L. W. "School Prayers and the Founding Fathers."
      Commentary 34 (September 1962): 225-230.

N79   Little, Lawrence Calvin. Religion and Public Education; a
      Bibliography. Pittsburgh: University of Pittsburgh, 1966.

N80   Loder, James E. Religion and the Public Schools. New York:
      Association Press, 1965.

N81   Lowry, Charles Wesley. To Pray or Not to Pray! Washington,
      D.C.: University Press of Washington, 1963.

N82   Madigan, L. M. "Religion in the Public School." Catholic
      World 189 (June 1959): 201-207.

N83   Mandel, Bernard. "Religion and the Public Schools of Ohio."
      Ohio State Archaeological and Historical Quarterly 58
      (1949): 185-206.

N84   McCluskey, Neil G. Public Schools and Moral Education.
      New York: Columbia University Press, 1958.

N85   McCollum, Vashti. One Woman's Fight. New York: Doubleday,
      1951.

N86   McCormick, Leo Joseph. Church-State Relationships in Education
      in Maryland. Washington, D.C.: Catholic University of
      America, 1942.

N87   McDevitt, Philip R. "How Bigotry was Kept Alive by Old-Time
      Textbooks." American Catholic Historical Society of
      Philadelphia Records 24 (September 1913): 251-261.

N88   McQuaid, B. J. The Public School Question. Boston: 1876.

N89   Madden, Ward. Religious Values in Education. New York:
      Harper, 1951.

N90   Mahoney, Charles J. The Relation of the State to Religious
      Education in Early New York, 1633-1825. Washington, D.C.:
      Catholic University of America, 1941.

N91   Mason, Robert E. Moral Values and Secular Education. New
      York: Columbia University Press, 1950.

N92   Mead, Edwin D. The Roman Catholic Church and the Public
      Schools. Boston: George H. Ellis, 1890.

N93   Menkus, B. "Evangelical Responsibility in Public Education."
      Christianity Today 15 (February 12, 1971): 10-12.

N94   Michaelsen, Robert. Piety in the Public School. New York:
      Macmillan, 1970.

N95   Miller, C. J. "Public School Bible Study: Sectarianism in
      Disguise." Christianity Today 13 (August 1, 1969): 3-5.

N96   Miller, E. O. "True Piety and the Regent's Prayer."
      Christian Century 79 (August 1, 1962): 934-936.

N97   Miller, William Lee. "Fight over America's Fourth R."
      Reporter 14 (March 22, 1956): 20-26.

N98   Moehlman, Conrad H. School and Church, the American Way.
      New York: Harper, 1944.

N99   Moore, Opal. Why Johnny Can't Learn. Milford, Michigan:
      Mott Media, 1975.

N100 Muir, William K. Prayer in the Public Schools. Chicago:
      University of Chicago, 1967. (New 1973 edition renamed
      Law and Attitude Change).

N101 National School Public Relations Association. Religion and
      the Schools. Washington, D.C.: 1970.

N102 Nations, Gilbert O. Roman Catholic War on Public Schools.
      Washington, D.C.: Independent Publishing Company, 1931.

N103 Newman, Louis. The Sectarian Invasion of Our Public Schools.
      San Francisco: 1925.

N104 Nielsen, Niels C. God in Education: A New Opportunity for
      American Schools. New York: Sheed and Ward, 1966.

N105 O'Neill, James M. The Catholic in Secular Education.
      New York: Longmans Green, 1956.

N106 Panoch, James U. and David L. Barr. Religion Goes to School.
      New York: Harper and Row, 1968.

N107 Pfeffer, Leo and William Ball. "Religion and the Court."
      Commonweal 76 (July 27, 1962): 417-422.

N108 Politella, Joseph. Religion in Education: An Annotated
      Bibliography. New York: Oneonta, 1956.

N109 Rainey, George S. Bibles in the Public Schools; or, a Plea
      for Religious Liberty. Otterbein, Indiana: 1924.

N110 Reilly, Daniel F. The School Controversy, 1891-1893.
      Washington, D.C.: Catholic University of America, 1943.

N111   Reutter, E. E. "Religion and Public Schools." Education
        Digest 39 (December 1973): 26-28.

N112   Rice, Charles E. The Supreme Court and Public Prayer.
        New York: Fordham University, 1964.

N113   Richardson, N. E. The Christ of the Classroom. New York:
        Macmillan, 1931.

N114   Rogers, V. M. "Are the Public Schools Godless?" Christian
        Century 74 (September 11, 1957): 1065-1067.

N115   Sheerin, John B. "Ban on Public School Prayer." Catholic
        World 195 (August 1962): 261-265.

N116   Sherwin, J. S. "Christmas in the Schools." School and
        Society 85 (November 9, 1957): 331-333.

N117   Sizer, Theodore R., ed. Religion and Public Education.
        Boston: Houghton Mifflin, 1967.

N118   Smith, Sherman M. Religious Education in Massachusetts.
        Syracuse: 1926.

N119   Steiner, Franklin. The Bible: Should it be in the School
        Room? The Question Considered Legally, Morally, and
        Religiously. Girard, Kansas: Haldeman-Julius, 1924.

N120   Swomley, John M. Religion, the State and the Schools.
        New York: Pegasus, 1968.

N121   Taft, Charles P. "Religion and the Public Schools."
        Christian Century 69 (August 20, 1952): 944-946.

N122   Thayer, V. T. The Attack upon the American Secular School.
        Boston: Beacon, 1951.

N123   Thayer, V. T. Religion in Public Education. New York:
        Viking, 1947.

N124   Tingelstad, Oscar A. Religious Element in American School
        Readers to 1850. Chicago: 1925.

N125   Towns, Elmer. Have the Public Schools Had It? Nashville:
        Thomas Nelson, 1974.

N126   Tyack, David. "The Kingdom of God and the Common School."
        Harvard Educational Review 36 (Fall 1966): 447-469.

N127   Van Dusen, Henry P. God in Education. New York: Scribners,
        1951.

N128   Warshaw, Thayer S. Religion, Education and the Supreme Court.
        Nashville: Abingdon, 1979.

SECTION O
CULTS, THE LAW AND RELIGIOUS FREEDOM

A new kind of religious conflict entered the American scene
in the 1970s and continues to pose serious problems for inter-
religious peace. That is the impact and challenge of new religious
movements, generally labeled cults by the long-established and
politically entrenched religions.

Opposition to the new religions has taken the form of coercion,
kidnapping and "deprogramming" - all in the name of combatting
alleged "brainwashing." The courts and the state and national
legislatures are the main battlegrounds for this new, yet in
many ways old, sectarian conflict.

For essential background reading one should begin with O8,
O29, O33, O56, and O65.

Strong criticisms of deprogramming and the fear that surrounds
it can be seen in O9, O57, O42 and O68.

Sympathetic studies of new religions include O20, O21, O12,
O28, and O70.

Hard-hitting, often hysterical, attacks on so-called cults
can be found in O7, O25, O31, O35, O36, O37, O44, O59, O60, O62
and O69.

O1 Appel, Willa. _Cults in America_. New York: Holt, Rinehart
    and Winston, 1983.

O2 Babbitt, Ellen M. "The Deprogramming of Religious Sect
    Members: A Private Right of Action Under Section 1985 (3)."
    Northwestern University Law Review 74 (1979): 229-254.

O3 Bainbridge, William, and Rodney Stark. "Sectarian Tension."
    Review of Religious Research 22 (1980): 105-124.

O4 Barker, Eileen, ed. _New Religious Movements: A Perspective
    for Understanding Society_. New York: Edwin Mellen Press,
    1982.

O5 Beckford, James A. "Politics and the Anti-Cult Movement."
    Annual Review of the Social Sciences of Religion 3
    (1979): 169-190.

O6 Bjornstad, James. _The Moon is not the Son_. Minneapolis:
    Dimension Books, 1976.

O7 Bjornstad, James. _Counterfeits at Your Door_. Glendale:
    Regal Books, 1979.

O8   Brandon, Thomas. New Religions, Conversions and Deprogram-
     ming: New Frontiers of Religious Liberty. Oak Park, Illinois:
     Center for Law and Religious Freedom, 1982.

O9   Bromley, David G. and Anson D. Sharpe. Strange Gods: The
     Great American Cult Scare. Boston: Beacon Press, 1981.

O10 Clark, J. Morris. "Guidelines for the Free Exercise Clause."
     Harvard Law Review 83 (1969): 327-365.

O11 Coleman, Lee, and Trudy Solomon. "Parens Patrie Treatment:
     Legal Punishment in Disguise." Hastings Constitutional
     Law Quarterly 3 (1976): 345-362.

O12 Cox, Harvey. Turning East. New York: Simon and Schuster, 1977.

O13 Davis, J. Michael. "Brainwashing: Fact, Fiction and Criminal
     Defense." University of Missouri Kansas City Law Review
     44 (1976): 438-479.

O14 Delgado, Richard A. "Limits to Proselytizing." Society
     17 (March-April 1980): 25-32.

O15 Delgado, Richard A. "Religious Totalism as Slavery." New
     York University Review of Law and Social Change 9 (1979-
     1980): 51-68.

O16 Delgado, Richard A. "Ascription of Criminal States of Mind:
     Toward a Defense Theory for the Coercively Persuaded ("Brain-
     washed") Defendant." Minnesota Law Review 63 (November
     1978): 1-34.

O17 Delgado, Richard A. "Religious Totalism: Gentle and Ungentle
     Persuasion Under the First Amendment." Southern California
     Law Review 51 (1977): 1-99.

O18 Dodge, Joseph. "The Free Exercise of Religion: A Socio-
     logical Approach." Michigan Law Review 67 (1969): 679-
     728.

O19 Dressler, Joshua. "Professor Delgado's Brainwashing Defense:
     Courting a Determinist Legal System." Minnesota Law Review
     63 (January 1979): 335-360.

O20 Ellwood, Robert S. Alternative Altars. Chicago: University
     of Chicago Press, 1979.

O21 Ellwood, Robert S. Religious and Spiritual Groups in
     Modern America. Englewood Cliffs: Prentice Hall, 1973.

O22 Enroth, Ronald, et.al. A Guide to Cults and New Religions.
     Downers Grove, Illinois: Intervarsity Press, 1983.

O23 Enroth, Ronald, et.al. The Lure of the Cults. Downers Grove,
     Illinois: Intervarsity Press, 1983.

024 Enroth, Ronald, ed., et al. The Lure of the Cults.
     Chappaqua: Christian Herald, 1979.

025 Enroth, Ronald. Youth, Brainwashing and the Extremist
     Cults. Grand Rapids: Zondervan, 1977.

026 Flowers, Ronald B. "Freedom of Religion Versus Civil
     Authority in Matters of Health." The Annals of the
     American Academy of Political and Social Science 446
     (November 1979): 149-162.

027 Garvey, John, ed. All our Sons and Daughters. Springfield,
     Illinois: Templegate Publishers, 1983.

028 Glock, Charles Y. and Robert N. Bellah. The New Religious
     Consciousness. Berkeley: University of California Press,
     1976.

029 Greene, Robert H. "People v. Religious Cult: Legal Guide-
     lines for Criminal Activities, Tort Liability, and Parental
     Remedies." Suffolk Law Review 11 (1977): 1025-1058.

030 Homer, David. "Abduction, Religious Sects and the Free
     Exercise Guarantee." Syracuse Law Review 25 (1974):
     623-645.

031 Hunt, Dave. The Cult Explosion. Irvine, California:
     Harvest House, 1980.

032 Johansen, R. B. and Sanford J. Rosen. "State and Local
     Regulation of Religious Solicitation of Funds: A
     Constitutional Perspective." The Annals of the American
     Academy of Political and Social Science 446 (November 1979):
     116-135.

033 LeMoult, John. "Deprogramming Members of Religious Sects."
     Fordham Law Review 46 (1978): 599-634.

034 Levine, Mark. "The Free Exercise Clause as a Defense to
     Involuntary Civil Commitment: Bringing Mental Illness
     into Religion." Albany Law Review 39 (1974): 144-156.

035 Levitt, Kent. Kidnapped for My Faith. Van Nuys, California:
     Bible Voice, 1978.

036 MacCollum, Joel A. Carnival of Souls. New York: Seabury
     Press, 1977.

037 Marten, Rachel. Escape. Denver: Accent Books, 1979.

038 Marten, Walter. The New Cults. Santa Ana, California:
     Vision House, 1980.

039 Omitted.

040   Needleman, Jacob and George Baker. Understanding the New
      Religions. New York: Seabury Press, 1978.

041   "Note. Conservatorships and Religious Cults: Divining a
      a Theory of Free Exercise." New York University Law
      Review 53 (1978): 1247-1289.

042   Pfeffer, Leo. "Equal Protection for Unpopular Sects."
      New York University Review of Law and Social Change
      9 (1979-1980): 9-16.

043   Pfeffer, Leo. "The Current State of the Law in the United
      States and the Separationist Agenda." The Annals of the
      American Academy of Political and Social Science 446
      (November 1979): 1-9.

044   Patrick, Ted and Tom Dulack. Let Our Children Go. New York:
      E. P. Dutton, 1976.

045   Patton, John E. The Case Against T M in the Schools.
      Grand Rapids: Baker Book House, 1976.

046   Pierson, Kit. "Cults, Deprogrammers, and the Necessity
      Defense." Michigan Law Review 80 (December 1981): 271-311.

047   Poythress, Norman G. "Behavior Modification, Brainwashing,
      Religion, and the Law." Journal of Religion and Health
      17 (1978): 238-243.

048   Robbins, Thomas. Civil Liberties, Brainwashing and Cults.
      Berkeley: Program for the Study of New Religious Movements,
      1979. (1981 revised edition).

049   Robbins, Thomas and Dick Anthony. "The Limits of Coercive
      Persuasion as an Explanation for Conversion to Authortarian
      Sects." Political Psychology 2 (Summer 1980): 23-30.

050   Robbins, Thomas. "Religious Movements, the State, and the
      Law: Reconceptualizing the Cult Problem." New York
      University Review of Law and Social Change 9 (1979-1980):
      33-49.

051   Rosenzweig, Charles. "High Demand Sects: Disclosure Legis-
      lation and the Free Exercise Clause." New England Law
      Review 15 (1979-1980): 128-159.

052   Rudin, James and Marcia Rudin. Prison or Paradise: The
      New Religious Cults. Philadelphia: Fortress Press, 1980.

053   Schuman, Eugene R. "Grand Jury Subpoenas and First Amendment
      Privileges." The Annals of the American Academy of Political
      and Social Science 446 (November 1979): 106-115.

054   Shapiro, Robert. "Mind Control or Intensity of Faith:
      The Constitutional Protection of Religious Beliefs."
      Harvard Civil Rights - Civil Liberties Law Review 13
      (1978): 751-797.

055   Shepherd, William C. "Legal Protection for Freedom of
      Religion." The Center Magazine 15 (March/April 1982):
      30-33.

056   Shepherd, William C. "The New Religions and the Religion of
      the Republic." Journal of the American Academy of Religion
      44 (1978): 509-525.

057   Shupe, Anson D. and David G. Bromley. The New Vigilantes.
      Beverly Hills: Sage Press, 1980.

058   Siegel, Terri I. "Deprogramming Religious Cultists."
      Loyola of Los Angeles Law Review 11 (September 1978):
      807-828.

059   Siegelman, Jim and Flo Conway. Snapping. Philadelphia:
      J. B. Lippincott Co., 1978.

060   Sparks, Jack. The Mindbenders: A Look at Current Cults.
      Nashville: Thomas Nelson, 1977.

061   Spendlove, Gretta. "Legal Issues in the Use of Guardianship
      Procedures to Remove Members of Cults." Arizona Law
      Review 18 (1976): 1095-1139.

062   Stoner, Carrol and Jo Anne Parke. All God's Children.
      Radnor, Pennsylvania: Chilton Book Co., 1977.

063   Whalen, William. Strange Gods. Huntington, Indiana:
      Our Sunday Visitor, 1981.

064   Weiss, Jonathan. "Privilege, Posture and Protection:
      Religion in the Law." Yale Law Journal 73 (1964):
      593-623.

065   Whelan, Charles M. "Governmental Attempts to Define Church
      and Religion." The Annals of the American Academy of
      Political and Social Science 446 (November 1979): 32-51.

066   Wogaman, J. Phillip. "The Churches and Legislative Advocacy."
      The Annals of the American Academy of Political and Social
      Science 446 (November 1979): 52-62.

067   Wood, James E., Jr. "Religion and Education: A Continuing
      Dilemma." The Annals of the American Academy of Political
      and Social Science 446 (November 1979): 63-77.

068   Worthing, Sharon L. "The State Takes Over a Church." Annals
      of the American Academy of Political and Social Science
      444 (November 1979):136-148.

069   Yamamoto, J. Isama.   The Puppet Master.   Downers Grove,
      Illinois: Intervarsity Press, 1977.

070   Zaretsky, Irving I. and Mark P. Leone.   Religious Movements
      in Contemporary America.   Princeton: Princeton University
      Press, 1974.

Note: An excellent new guide to 1,001 sources in this area was
published by Garland Publishing Inc. in 1984 and entitled
The Anti-Cult Movement in America: a Bibliographic History by
Anson D. Shupe Jr., David G. Bromley and Donna L. Oliver.

SECTION P
CIVIL RELIGION

Every nation has a kind of civil religion, an almost inde-
finable ethic of shared values which somehow define its indentity.
This is no less true of the United States.

Our civil religion takes many forms: Presidential prayer
proclamations and annual Prayer Breakfasts, paid chaplaincies
in Congress and the armed forces, religious rituals at Presidential
inaugurations.

Still, the concept seems elusive. Some define civil religion
as the use of religion for political ends. Some see it as a
danger to the republic. Others see it as a subtle danger to the
integrity and authenticity of genuine religious experience, a
salute which politicians pay to the religions.

Some seminal attempts to define the subject include P4-P7,
P16, P20, P28, P31, P44, P45.

The religious views of our Presidents are explored by P2,
P4, P8, P13, P14, P15, P18, P19, P22, P24, P26, P27, P34.

Some critical looks at the abuses of civil religion are
found in P35, P39, P21.

P1   Ahlstrom, Sydney E. "Requiem for Patriotic Piety." Worldview
     15 (August 1972): 9-11.

P2   Alley, Robert S. So Help Me God: Religion and the Presidency,
     Wilson to Nixon. Richmond: John Knox Press, 1972.

P3   Palitzer, Alfred. "Some Thoughts About Civil Religion."
     Journal of Church and State 16 (Winter 1974): 31-50.

P4   Bellah, Robert N. "American Civil Religion in the 1970s."
     Anglican Theological Review Supplementary Series No. 1
     55 (July 1973): 8-20.

P5   Bellah, Robert N. "Civil Religion in America." Daedalus
     96 (Winter 1967): 1-25.

P6   Bellah, Robert N. The Broken Covenant: American Civil
     Religion in Time of Trial. New York: Seabury Press, 1975.

P7   Bellah, Robert N. and Philip E. Hammond. Varieties of Civil
     Religion. San Francisco: Harper and Row, 1980.

P8   Bonnell, John Sutherland. Presidential Profiles: Religion
     in the Life of American Presidents. Philadelphia: Westminster
     Press, 1971.

P9   Bowden, Henry Warner. "A Historian's Response to the Con-
      cept of American Civil Religion." Journal of Church and
      State 17 (Autumn 1975): 495-505.

P10   Bryant, M. Darrol. "Beyond Messianism: Toward a New
      American Civil Religion." The Ecumenist 11 (May-June
      1973): 49-51.

P11   Cherry, Conrad, ed. God's New Israel: Religious Inter-
      pretations of American Destiny. Englewood Cliffs: Prentice-
      Hall, 1971.

P12   Cherry, Conrad. "Nation, Church and Private Religion: The
      Emergence of an American Pattern." Journal of Church and
      State 14 (Spring 1972): 223-233.

P13   Cousins, Norman. In God We Trust: The Religious Beliefs
      and Ideas of the American Founding Fathers. New York:
      Harper, 1958.

P14   Flowers, Ronald B. "President Jimmey Carter, Evangelicalism,
      Church-State Relations and Civil Religion." Journal of
      Church and State 25 (Winter 1983): 113-132.

P15   Fuller, Edmund and David E. Green. God in the White House:
      The Faiths of American Presidents. New York: Crown, 1968.

P16   Garrett, James Leo, Jr. "Civil Religion: Clarifying the
      Semantic Problem." Journal of Church and State 16
      (Spring 1974): 187-195.

P17   Greeley, Andrew. "The Civil Religion of Ethnic Americans."
      Worldview 16 (February 1973): 21-27.

P18   Gustafson, Merlin. "President Hoover and the National
      Religion." Journal of Church and State 16 (Winter 1974):
      85-100.

P19   Hampton, Vernon B. The Religious Background of the White
      House. New York: Christopher, 1932.

P20   Hardy, Robert T. "A Decisive Turn in the Civil Religion
      Debate." Theology Today 37 (October 1980): 342-350.

P21   Hatfield, Mark. "Piety and Patriotism." Church Herald
      30 (March 23, 1973): 4-6.

P22   Henderson, Charles P. The Nixon Theology. New York:
      Harper and Row, 1972.

P23   Hudson, Winthrop S., ed. Nationalism and Religion in America:
      Concepts of American Identity and Mission. New York:
      Harper and Row, 1970.

P24 Isely, Bliss. <u>Presidents, Men of Faith</u>. Boston: Wilde, 1953.

P25 Jewett, Robert. <u>The Captain America Complex: The Dilemma of Zealous Nationalism</u>. Philadelphia: Westminster Press, 1973.

P26 La Fontaine, Charles V. "God and Nation in Selected U.S. Presidential and Inaugural Addresses, 1789-1945." <u>Journal of Church and State</u> 18 (Winter 1976): 39-60; (Autumn 1976): 503-521.

P27 Linder, Robert. "Reagan at Kansas State: Civil Religion in the Service of the New Right." <u>The Reformed Journal</u> 32 (December 1982): 13-15.

P28 Linder, Robert D. "Civil Religion in Historical Perspective." <u>Journal of Church and State</u> 17 (Autumn 1975): 399-421.

P29 Linder, Robert D. and Richard V. Pierard. <u>The Twilight of the Saints: Biblical Christianity and Civil Religion in America</u>. Downers Grove: Intervarsity Press, 1978.

P30 Marty, Martin E. "The Status of Societal Religion in the United States." <u>Concordia Theological Monthly</u> 36 (November 1965): 687-705.

P31 Mead, Sidney E. "The Nation with the Soul of a Church." <u>Church History</u> 36 (September 1967): 262-283.

P32 Mead, Sidney E. <u>The Nation with the Soul of a Church</u>. New York: Harper and Row, 1975.

P33 Mead, Sidney E. <u>The Old Religion in the Brave New World: Reflections on the Relation Between Christendom and the Republic</u>. Berkeley: University of California Press, 1980.

P34 Menendez, Albert J. "The President as Preacher." <u>Church and State</u> 35 (May 1982): 13-17.

P35 Miller, William Lee. <u>Piety Along the Potomac</u>. Boston: Houghton Mifflin, 1964.

P36 Nagel, Paul C. <u>The Sacred Trust: American Nationality, 1798-1898</u>. New York: Oxford University Press, 1971.

P37 Neuhaus, Richard. "The War, the Churches and Civil Religion." <u>The Annals of the American Academy of Political and Social Science</u> 387 (January 1970): 128-140.

P38 Richey, Russell E. and Donald S. Jones, eds. <u>American Civil Religion</u>. New York: Harper and Row, 1974.

P39 Rose, Stephen C. "Culture Religion: Competition to Christian Faith." <u>Social Action</u> 37 (February 1971): 8-9.

P40   Smith, Elwyn A., ed. The Religion of the Republic.
      Philadelphia: Fortress Press, 1970.

P41   Smith, Kalmin D. "The Politics of Civil Religion." The
      American Benedictine Review 26 (March 1975): 89-106.

P42   Smylie, John Edwin. "The Christian Church and National
      Ethics." Theology Today 20 (October 1963): 313-321.

P43   Stauffer, Robert E. "Civil Religion, Technocracy and the
      Private Sphere." Journal for the Scientific Study of
      Religion 13 (1974): 415-425.

P44   Strout, Cushing. The New Heavens and New Earth: Political
      Religion in America. New York: Harper and Row, 1975.

P45   Tuveson, Ernest Lee. Redeemer Nation: The Idea of America's
      Milerrial Role. Chicago: University of Chicago Press, 1968.

P46   Williams, Colin, et al. The Changing Nature of America's
      Civil Religion. Aspen: Aspen Institute for Humanistic
      Studies, 1973.

Addendum

P47   Boller, Paul F. "Religion and the U.S. Presidency."
      Journal of Church and State 21 (Winter 1979): 5-21.

SECTION Q
THE NEW CHRISTIAN RIGHT, THE 1980 ELECTION,
AND THE REAGAN PRESIDENCEY

The contemporary revival of political conflict along
religious lines can be traced to the backlash of embittered
conservative Protestants since the mid-1970s, beginning even
before Jimmy Carter's election. But the eruption of a new
debate over the role of religion in public life began in earnest
during the 1980 Presidential election, when crusaders for a
fundamentalist restoration contributed significantly to Ronald
Reagan's election.

The Reagan Administration's policies on church-state issues
represent the greatest departure from the American norm in this
century. Hence, much of the debate over the parameters of
"morality" has come in response to its policies.

Spokespersons for the Christian Right sound forth in Q6,
Q7, Q18, Q22, Q23, Q27, Q29, Q42-44, Q68, Q69, Q73-76, Q80-84,
Q88, Q92-95.

Critics of the movement are numerous. They include Q1,
Q5, Q11, Q12, Q15, Q16, Q17, Q20, Q21, Q24, Q26, Q32, Q35, Q36,
Q40, Q51, Q55, Q77, Q78, Q86, Q87, Q90, Q99.

Some relatively dispassionate but at least partially critical
views are expressed by Q3, Q14, Q28, Q47, Q54, Q60, Q63, Q64, Q89,
Q96, Q97, Q101.

Some straight-forward analyses of the 1980 election include
Q8, Q10, Q19, Q33, Q37, Q48, Q57, Q58, Q59, Q61, Q71, Q85.

Q1   Alley, Robert S. and Irby B. Brown. "The Moral Monopoly."
     Emmy 3 (Winter 1981): 35-36.

Q2   Anderson, Jim, et al. "The Moral Majority: Judgment on
     Liberal Churches." Alban Institute Action Information
     7 (May-June 1981): 1-4.

Q3   Bennett, John C. "Assessing the Concerns of the Religious
     Right." Christian Century 98 (October 14, 1981): 1018-1022.

Q4   Berger, Peter. "The Class Struggle in American Religion."
     Christian Century 98 (February 25, 1981): 194-199.

Q5   Bollier, David. Liberty and Justice for Some: Defending
     a Free Society from the Radical Right's Holy War on
     Democracy. New York: Ungar, 1982.

Q6   Brown, Harold O. J. "The Road to Theocracy?" National
     Review 32 (October 31, 1980): 1328-1329.

Q7   Brown, Harold O. J. The Reconstruction of the Republic.
      New Rochelle: Arlington House, 1977.

Q8   Castelli, Jim. "The Religious Vote." Commonweal 107
      (November 21, 1980): 650-651.

Q9   Cattani, Richard. "Political Science Elites." Public
      Opinion 4 (1981): 50-54.

Q10   Cerillo, Augustus. "Pentecostals and the Presidential
      Election." Agora 4 (Winter 1981): 2-4.

Q11   Chapman, Alan. Thunder on the Right. New York: Pantheon,
      1980.

Q12   Clabaugh, Gary. Thunder on the Right: The Protestant
      Fundamentalists. Chicago: Nelson Hall, 1974.

Q13   Clouse, G. Robert, ed. The Cross and the Flag. Carve
      Stream: Creation House, 1972.

Q14   Conn, Joseph L. "The New Christian Politics." Church and
      State 33 (July/August 1980): 14-22.

Q15   Conway, Flo and Jim Siegelman. Holy Terror. New York:
      Doubleday, 1982.

Q16   Cooper, John Charles. Religious Pied Pipers: A Critique
      of Radical Right-Wing Religion. Valley Forge: Judson
      Press, 1981.

Q17   Cooper, John Charles. The Turn Right. Philadelphia:
      Westminster Press, 1970.

Q18   Cotham, Perry C. Politics, Americanism and Christianity.
      Grand Rapids: Baker Book House, 1976.

Q19   Denier, Greg. "A Shift Toward the Right? or a Failure on
      the Left?" Christianity and Crisis 40 (December 22, 1980):
      355-360.

Q20   Ericson, Edward L. American Freedom and the Radical Right.
      New York: Frederick Ungar, 1982.

Q21   Fackre, Gabriel. The Religious Right and the Christian
      Faith. Grand Rapids: Eerdmans, 1982.

Q22   Falwell, Jerry. Listen America. New York: Doubleday, 1980.

Q23   Felsenthal, Carol. The Sweetheart of the Silent Majority.
      New York: Doubleday, 1981.

Q24   Finch, Phillip. God, Guts and Guns: A Close Look at the
      Radical Right. New York: Seaview/Putnam, 1983.

Q25 Frazier, Claude A., ed. <u>Religion and Politics Can Mix</u>. Nashville: Broadman, 1974.

Q26 Goodman, William R. and James T. H. Price. <u>Jerry Falwell: An Unauthorized Profile</u>. Lynchburg: Paris and Associates, 1981.

Q27 Hargis, Billy James. <u>Why I Fight for a Christian America</u>. Nashville: Thomas Nelson, 1974.

Q28 Hastey, Stan and Warner Ragsdale. "Right Religion, Right Politics?" <u>Home Missions</u> 51 (September-October 1980): 67-72.

Q29 Helms, Jesse. <u>Where Free Man Shall Stand</u>. Grand Rapids: Zondervan, 1976.

Q30 Henry, Paul. <u>Politics for Evangelicals</u>. Valley Forge: Judson Press, 1974.

Q31 Higgins, George C. "The Prolife Movement and the New Right." <u>America</u> 143 (September 13, 1980): 107-110.

Q32 Hill, Samuel S. and Dennis E. Owen. <u>The New Religious-Political Right in America</u>. Nashville: Abingdon, 1982.

Q33 Himmelfarb, Milton. "Are Jews Becoming Republican?" <u>Commentary</u> 72 (August 1981): 27-31.

Q34 Hunter, J. D. "The Young Evangelicals and the New Class." <u>Review of Religious Research</u> 22 (1980): 155-169.

Q35 Jorstad, Erling. <u>The Politics of Moralism: The New Christian Right in American Life</u>. Minneapolis: Augsburg, 1981.

Q36 Kater, John L. <u>Christians on the Right</u>. New York: Seabury Press, 1982.

Q37 Keller, Bill. "Evangelical Conservatives Move from Pews to Polls." <u>Congressional Quarterly Weekly Report</u> 38 (September 6, 1980): 2627-2634.

Q38 Kirkpatrick, Jeane J. "Politics and the New Class." <u>Society</u> 16 (January 1979): 42-48.

Q39 Kockey, Jonathan Martin. <u>The New Right 1960-1968 with Epilogue 1969-1980</u>. Lanham: University Press of America, 1983.

Q40 Krauthammer, Charles. "The Humanist Phantom: A Clash of Ignorant Armies." <u>New Republic</u> 185 (July 25, 1981): 20-25.

Q41 Ladd, Everett Carll. "The New Lines are Drawn: Class and Ideology in America." <u>Public Opinion</u> 1 (August 1978): 48-53.

Q42   La Haye, Tim. The Battle for the Mind. Old Tappan: Revell,
      1980.

Q43   La Haye, Tim. The Battle for the Family. Old Tappan: Revell,
      1982.

Q44   La Haye, Tim. The Battle for the School. Old Tappan: Revell,
      1983.

Q45   Lichter, Linda S., et al. "Hollywood and America: The Odd
      Couple." Public Opinion 5 (1983): 54-58.

Q46   Lichter, S. Robert and Stanley Rothman. "Media and Business
      Elites." Public Opinion 4 (1982): 42-47.

Q47   Liebman, Robert and Robert Wuthnow, eds. The New Christian
      Right. Hawthorne: Aldine, 1983.

Q48   Lipset, Seymour Martin and Earl Robb. "The Election and the
      Evangelicals." Commentary 71 (March 1981): 25-31.

Q49   Lipset, Seymour Martin. "The New Class and the Professoriate."
      Society 16 (January 1979): 31-38.

Q50   Lorentzen, Louise J. "Evangelical Life Style Concerns Expressed
      in Political Action." Sociological Analysis 41 (Summer 1980):
      144-154.

Q51   Maguire, Daniel C. The New Subversives: Anti-Americanism
      of the Religious Right. New York: Crossroads, 1982.

Q52   Mann, Thomas E. and Norman J. Ornstein. "Election '82."
      Public Opinion 5 (1983): 6-12.

Q53   Martin, William. "God's Angry Man." Texas Monthly 9
      (April 1981): 152-157, 223-236.

Q54   Marty, Martin E. "Twelve Points to Consider about the New
      Christian Right." Context 12 (July 15, 1980): 1-5.

Q55   McIntyre, Thomas J. The Fear Brokers. Boston: Beacon Press,
      1979.

Q56   Menendez, Albert J. "Anti-Catholicism in the '80s: Is it
      Heating Up?" Liberty 79 (January/February 1984): 4-7.

Q57   Menendez, Albert J. "Church, State and the 1980 Presidential
      Race." Church and State 33 (January 1980): 6-9.

Q58   Menendez, Albert J. "Religion and Presidential Politics 1980."
      Worldview 22 (November 1979): 11-14.

Q59 Menendez, Albert J. "Religion at the Polls, 1980."
     Church and State 33 (December 1980): 15-18.

Q60 Mouw, Richard J. "Assessing the Moral Majority." Reformed
     Journal 31 (June 1981): 13-15.

Q61 Neusner, Jacob. "How Should Jews Vote?" National Review
     32 (October 17, 1980): 1250-1252.

Q62 "Opinion Roundup." Public Opinion 5 (1983): 21-41.

Q63 Pierard, Richard V. "The New Religious Right: A Formidable
     Force in American Politics." Choice 19 (March 1982):
     865-879.

Q64 Pierard, Richard V. "Reagan and the Evangelicals." The
     Christian Century 100 (December 21, 1983): 1182-1185.

Q65 Pines, Burton Yale. Back to Basics. New York: William
     Morrow & Company, 1982.

Q66 Pines, Burton Yale. "A Majority for Morality?" Public
     Opinion 4 (April 1981): 42-47.

Q67 Plissner, Martin and Warren Mitofsky. "Political Elites."
     Public Opinion 4 (April 1981): 47-50.

Q68 Price, John. America at the Crossroads. Wheaton: Tyndale
     House, 1976.

Q69 "The Pro-Family Movement." Conservative Digest 9 (May-June
     1980): 14-24.

Q70 Religion in America, 1982. Princeton: Religion Research
     Center, 1982.

Q71 Ribuffo, Leo P. "Fundamentalism Revisited: Liberals and
     That Old-Time Religion." The Nation 231 (November 29,
     1980): 570-573.

Q72 Roberts, James. The Conservative Decade. Westport:
     Arlington House, 1980.

Q73 Robison, James. Save America to Save the World. Wheaton:
     Tyndale House, 1980.

Q74 Rowe, H. Edward. Save America. Old Tappan: Revell, 1976.

Q75 Schaeffer, Francis A. A Christian Manifesto. Westchester,
     Illinois: Crossway Books, 1981.

Q76 Schaeffer, Franky. A Time for Anger: The Myth of Neutrality.
     Westchester, Illinois: Crossway Books, 1982.

Q77   Shinn, Roger L. "Moral Majority: Distorting Faith and
      Patriotism." A.D. 10 (August 1981): 13-15.

Q78   Shriver, Peggy L. The Bible Vote: Religion and the New
      Right. New York: Pilgrim Press, 1981.

Q79   Stackhouse, Max L. "Religious Right." Commonweal 109
      (January 24, 1982): 52-56.

Q80   Stanley, Charles F. Stand Up America. Atlanta: In Touch
      Ministries, 1980.

Q81   Strober, Jerry and Ruth Tomczak. Jerry Falwell: Aflame
      for God. Nashville: Nelson, 1979.

Q82   Sweating, George. Is America Dying? Chicago: Moody, 1974.

Q83   Sweating, George. A National Call to Renewal. Chicago:
      Moody, 1976.

Q84   Thomas, Cal. Book Burning. Westchester, Illinois: Crossway
      Books, 1983.

Q85   "Tide of Born-Again Politics." Newsweek 100 (September 15,
      1980): 28-36.

Q86   Vetter, Herbert F., ed. Speak Out Against the New Right.
      Boston: Beacon Press, 1982.

Q87   Wallis, Jim and Wes Michaelson. "The Plan to Save America:
      A Disclosure of an Alarming Political Initiative by the
      Evangelical Far Right." Sojourners 5 (April 1976): 4-12.

Q88   Walton, Rus. One Nation Under God. Old Tappan: Revell, 1975.

Q89   Webber, Robert. The Moral Majority: Right of Wrong?
      Westchester, Illinois: Crossway Books, 1981.

Q90   "What's Wrong with Born-Again Politics?" Christian Century
      97 (October 22, 1980): 1002-1004

Q91   Whitaker, Robert W., ed. The New Right Papers. New York:
      St. Martin's, 1982.

Q92   Whitehead, John W. The Second American Revolution. Elgin,
      Illinois: David C. Cook, 1982.

Q93   Whitehead, John W. The Separation Illusion. Milford,
      Michigan: Mott Media, 1977.

Q94   Whitehead, John W. The Stealing of America. Westchester,
      Illinois: Crossway Books, 1983.

Q95   Willoughby, William.   Does America Need the Moral Majority?
      Plainfield: Haven Books, 1981.

Q96   Wood, James E., Jr.   "Religious Fundamentalism and the New
      Right."   Journal of Church and State 22 (Autumn 1980):
      409-421.

Q97   Wood, James E., Jr.   Religion and Politics.   Waco: Baylor
      University Press, 1983.

Q98   Yankelovich, Daniel.   "Stepchildren of the Moral Majority."
      Psychology Today 16 (November 1981): 5-6.

Q99   Young, Perry Deane.   God's Bullies.   New York: Holt, Rinehart
      and Winston, 1982.

Q100 Zwier, Robert and Richard Smith.   "Christian Politics and
      the New Right."   Christian Century 97 (October 8, 1980):
      937-941.

Q101 Zwier, Robert.   Born-Again Politics: The New Christian
      Right in America.   Downers Grove: Intervarsity Press, 1982.

AUTHOR INDEX

Abbey, Sue Wilson E55
Abel, Theodore L164
Adams, Elizabeth Laura L1
Adams, James L. G1, K1
Adams, Marjorie E. N1
Ahlstrom, Sydney E. P1
Aldama, Manuel L165
Alexander, Charles C. E56, E57, E58, E59
Allen, Lee N. H1, H2
Allies, Thomas William L2
Allensmith, Wesley and Beverly H3
Alley, Robert S. P2, Q1
Altfeld, E. Milton B1
Amand de Mendieta, Emmanuel L166
Ander, Fritiof D1
Anderson, Elin F1
Anderson, Jim Q2
Angell, Charles L3
Anson, Peter Frederick L4
Appel, Willa O1
Angle, Paul M. E60
Armstrong, April Ousler L5
Arrien, Rose Fe L167
Atchison, Carla Joan D2
Autry, Allen Hill E1
Avin, Benjamin H. E61

Babbitt, Ellen M. O2
Baggaley, Andrew R. I1
Bain, J.A. L168
Bainbridge, William O3
Baker, Gladys L6
Baker, James T. K2
Baker, Jean H. C1
Baker, Robert A. J1
Balitzer, Alfred P3
Ball, William B. M1, M2, N6
Ballantyne, Murray L7
Baltazar, E.R. N7
Barker, Eileen O4
Barnhouse, Donald Grey J2

Barnum, Samuel W. D3
Barreau, Jean Claude L8
Barres, Oliver L9
Barrett, E. Boyd E2, L10
Barrett, Patricia J3, J4
Barrois, G.A. L229
Barry, Colman J. C2
Barry, John Paul C3
Bartell, Ernest M3
Battersby, Sister Agnes C. C4
Baughin, William A. C5
Baum, D. H4
Bayly, Joseph M4
Bayssiere, Pierre L169
Beach, Fred Francis M5
Beals, Carleton C6
Bean, William G. C7, C8
Bechtel, William R. F2
Beck, Walter H. M6
Beckford, James A. O5
Beckman, Robert E. C9
Bedsole, Adolph N8
Beggs, David W. N9
Bellah, Robert N. P4, P5, P6, P7
Belloc, Hilaire E3
Beman, Lamar Taney N10
Benjamin, Marge M7
Bennett, A.H. L11
Bennett, John C. J5, Q3
Benson, Peter L. H5
Benson, Robert Hugh L12
Bentley, Max E62, E63
Berger, Max C10
Berger, Peter Q4
Bernarding, Peter J. L230
Bianchi, Eugene C. J6
Billington, Ray Allen C11, C12, C13
Birdwhistell, Ira V. K3
Bishop, Claire Huchet M8
Bishop, L.K. F5
Bjornstad, James O6, O7
Blanchette, Charles Alphonse L170